The
Do's & ~~Don'ts~~
of Delightful
Dieting

by
Arthur S. Donellen

Foreword by
Sidney G. Page, Jr., M.D.

Westover
Publishing Company

A Media General Publication

INTRODUCTION

Most of us believe that dieting is a bore at best, torture at worst. Generally speaking, we are correct. I've read and tried a number of diets, and many of them will do the job — if they don't drive you stark raving mad first. But the diet regimen in this book is neither tedious nor torturous. I know; I've used it frequently, and considering my proclivity for food, if I can stand it (and even enjoy it) anyone can. Like anything else worthwhile, it does require some discipline, but it is much less stringent than any other with which I am familiar.

The Do's and Don'ts of Delightful Dieting is based on a diet that Dr. Sidney G. Page, Jr., my friend and my physician, has been prescribing to his patients for some twenty-five years. It calls for a calorie intake of 1,000 a day, give or take a few. There are a wide variety of foods allowed, and they are fairly evenly distributed during the day.

Many other diet books offer crash programs; this one does not; it's strictly up to you. Using it, you can lose from three to five pounds per week. Once you reach your desired weight, you can relax and splurge if you wish. If the body can only *lose* so much per day, then it makes sense that it can only *gain* a certain amount in the same period. So when you want to eat, drink, party or go on a holiday, do it. Then, if the scales show your weight has gone up a few pounds, all you have to do is go back on the diet again, until your weight is back to where you want it. After all, no one wants to go through life with the bleak prospect of never being able to indulge in that hot fudge sundae once in a while. The splurge, however, should be all at once, preferably in a single day rather than spread over several days. The penalty for such a fall off the wagon is entirely painless, as proven by the one-hundred daily menus in this book.

To make this diet most effective, you should eat everything on the "required foods" list. Don't skip meals, and don't fast during the day so you can gorge at dinnertime. The diet just won't work that way. And you must stay away from alcohol.

Once you get through the discipline of the first several days, you should feel that you're eating in a completely normal way. You should not experience any weakness, since the foods prescribed offer ample nutrition; and you shouldn't particularly crave foods you cannot have, since the diet offers a wide variety of tasty gourmet treats.

There are, of course, countless ways of varying the daily diet while still maintaining the 1,000-calorie limit that is guaranteed to take away unwanted excess pounds. The menus in the book are examples of gourmet meals that add nutrition, strength, and vitality to the dieter while at the same time providing interesting, provocative, and well-balanced combinations on a long-term basis. For my money, and hopefully for yours, that's about as much as a diet can offer.

A. S. D.

A WORD FROM DOCTOR SIDNEY G. PAGE, JR.

We are fortunate to be living in a land of plenty, but because of this, many patients through the years find themselves putting on unwanted, unhealthy extra pounds. When this occurs they must first get rid of the excess fat at a steady pace and they must also eat balanced meals. Once the desired weight is achieved, they must then monitor their eating habits so that they keep their slimness. The best way of doing this is to avoid a major overload at any one meal and to count calories.

The term "calorie" is a simple one. The body gets its energy from the fuel contained in food. A calorie is a measure of that fuel, just as a watt is a measure of electrical power. If the food you eat supplies more fuel (calories) than your body needs to burn in order to get the energy it requires, the excess fuel (calories) is turned into body fat and stored away.

Fad diets can be dangerous. Some are so monotonous that they are almost impossible to stay with for any period of time. Others are dangerous because they rob the body of needed nutrients. For anyone undertaking a diet, it is recommended that they be given a physical checkup by their family doctor.

The menus provided in this book are so unusually generous that you must count your calories as honestly as you do the points in a game, being faithful both to sizes and to measurements. These well-balanced, high-vitamin, high-mineral menus for delicious full-course meals are designed for people who love to eat. They are rich in everything except fat-producing calories. You will notice that your daily selection of foods includes the following:

- Citrus fruit juice or tomato juice
- 1 other fresh fruit
- A raw vegetable salad
- 1 egg (if you are allergic to eggs,
      substitute cheese or more skim milk
      or meat of approximately equal
      calories)
- At least 1 serving of meat, fish, or fowl
- A cooked green leafy vegetable
- 1 potato, preferably baked
- Butter or margarine
- 1 pint of skim milk or buttermilk (as a beverage or in cooking)

In addition to calorie counting, there are some rules that must be followed:

Do not eat between meals. You may replace the skim milk allowed at meals with coffee or tea, and drink the skim milk in mid-afternoon and at bedtime.

Limit your total number of sleeping hours to 8 at the very most in any 24-hour period. Take no salt, except that used in cooking. Include liver or other organ meat in your menu at least once weekly. Eat no fried foods at all. In cooking, you may substitute oil for butter or margarine, remembering that 1 tablespoon of oil is 125 calories, while 1 tablespoon of butter is 100 and therefore you must subtract from your daily allowance accordingly.

Be careful of artificial sweeteners. Saccharin is harmless, but it should not be cooked with other ingredients. Saccharin tablets should be crushed and dissolved and added after heating is complete.

The use of mineral oil is strictly forbidden. It has been proven that this oil absorbs and carries out of the system certain vitamins which are extremely important to health and especially so during the weight reduction program.

Do not drink any beverages while you are actually eating your food. Drink your skim milk either before you begin your meal or after you have finished. Drink all the water, black coffee, or tea that you want — but do it between meals.

Do not skip meals. Do not shift a part of one menu to another menu for later in the day. Eat every article of food shown on every menu and in the quantities specified. Remember, when the body is poorly fed it becomes sullen. It rebelliously slows down all of its processes and stubbornly holds on to the fat instead of burning it up.

Weigh yourself only once weekly and always on the same scale. Do it in the morning just before dressing. Don't be discouraged when from time to time your scales don't show the amount of fat you are losing. With many people, the body sometimes retains water to take the place of lost fat. However, in a couple of weeks (sometimes sooner) such accumulation of water will suddenly be excreted and then the scales will show that you had actually been losing body fat all the time! Salt is another thing that causes the unnatural accumulation of water in the tissues, so the less salt used in cooking, the less you will be bothered by water retention.

The menus in this book, if properly followed, will lead anyone to healthy and happy slimness and at the same time provide the body with the nutrition it needs for a vigorous life.

Use this book only when you want to lose three pounds a week. The theory behind this book is that you can only gain so much in a given day and you can only lose so much in a given day. The only thing to remember is not to slip when you are on the diet. If you want to splurge, do it in a 24-hour period only and then go back to the diet. It is a comfortable diet with enormous variation. It is not a monotonous diet. It is a nutritionally good diet and provides no problems for the human body.

ABOUT THE MENUS AND CALORIE COUNTS

Calorie charts vary in much the same way that ideal weight charts do. We have chosen to use the calorie chart that has been successful through the years with Dr. Page's patients, but have also referred to the latest calorie counts of the U.S. Department of Agriculture. You will find that 50 calories for a baked potato means that the potato is very small (5 to a pound), but there is a bonus if you eat the skin. Always remember to thoroughly wash the skin of the potato before baking. If you can get the new red skin potatoes, substitute one boiled for the baked potato.

In general, we have not counted calories for foods having less than 5. Lemon and lime juice or a small amount of chopped onion or cucumber do count for a little something, but it just isn't practical to worry about such insignificant numbers. Many of the combination recipes include several of the daily food requirements. An example of this is Fish Pie (280 calories) which has cooked onions, pepper, margarine, milk, fish, and it is topped with mashed potatoes.

You will see "Tossed Green Salad," or "Mixed Green Salad," (call them what you wish) used throughout the menus. Feel free to use your imagination in combining the following ingredients for a green salad bowl, a tossed green salad, or a combination:

GREENS	OTHER INGREDIENTS
Lettuce	Chopped onion
Young spinach	Chopped dill pickle
Endive	Tomato wedges
Romaine	Capers
Shredded cabbage	Sliced radishes
Watercress	Diced celery
Escarole	Sliced cucumber
	Chopped green pepper
	Shredded raw parsnip
	Small pieces of raw cauliflower

For dressings, use low calorie commercial dressing, Vinegar Dressing,* Tangy Seafood Cocktail Sauce,* Lemon-Caper Sauce,* Barbecue Dressing,* Tomato Juice Dressing,* Spiced Vinegar* or Dr. Page's Delight Salad Dressing.* A green salad with any of these dressings is 15 to 18 calories.

---

* This symbol indicates that the recipe is detailed elsewhere in this book.

101
Menus
and
Calorie
Counts

TOTAL CALORIES: 1000

BREAKFAST

	Serving	Calories
Pear (canned in syrup)	2 halves	75
Rice Krispies	¾ cup	81
Sugar	1 teaspoon	16
Skim Milk	1 cup	88
Coffee or Tea (black or with artificial sweetener)	1 cup	—
	TOTAL	260

LUNCH

	Serving	Calories
Clam-Tomato Cocktail*	1 serving	12
Bologna	1 slice	25
Boiled Ham	1 slice	100
Cottage Cheese	¼ cup	60
Deviled Eggs*	2 halves	75
Melba Toast	1 slice	16
Skim Milk	1 cup	88
	TOTAL	376

DINNER

	Serving	Calories
Ovenburgers*	1 serving	165
Baked Potato	1	50
Butter or Margarine	1 pat	76
Broccoli	½ cup	37
Tomato Aspic Salad*	1 serving	30
Raw Celery	2 inner stalks	6
Coffee or Tea (black or with artificial sweetener)	1 cup	—
	TOTAL	364

TOTAL CALORIES: 995

BREAKFAST

	Serving	Calories
Grapefruit	½ medium	60
Scrambled Egg*	1	76
Toast	1 slice	75
Butter or Margarine	½ pat	38
Skim Milk	1 cup	88
Coffee or Tea (black or with artificial sweetener)	1 cup	—
	TOTAL	**337**

LUNCH

	Serving	Calories
Pan-Broiled Liver*	1 serving	138
Baked Potato	1	50
Diet Sour Cream*	1 tablespoon	20
Green Beans	½ cup	22
Fresh Apricot	1	28
Coffee or Tea (black or with artificial sweetener)	1 cup	—
	TOTAL	**258**

DINNER

	Serving	Calories
Fish Pie*	1 serving	280
Broccoli with Mustard Dill Sauce*	1 serving	80
Tossed Green Salad	1 cup	15
Vinegar Dressing*		—
Lemon Mist*	1 serving	25
Coffee or Tea (black or with artificial sweetener)	1 cup	—
	TOTAL	**400**

TOTAL CALORIES: 1013

BREAKFAST

	Serving	Calories
Pineapple Juice (canned)	½ cup	54
Shirred Egg*	1	100
Toast	1 slice	75
Butter or Margarine	½ pat	38
Skim Milk	1 cup	88
Coffee or Tea (black or with artificial sweetener)	1 cup	—
	TOTAL	355

LUNCH

	Serving	Calories
Chicken Gumbo Soup*	1 cup	25
Ry-Krisp (seasoned and toasted)	2 triple crackers	50
Tossed Green Salad	1 cup	15
Lemon Caper Sauce*		—
Skim Milk Custard*	1 serving	135
Fresh Strawberries	½ cup	41
Coffee or Tea (black or with artificial sweetener)	1 cup	—
	TOTAL	266

DINNER

	Serving	Calories
Meat Balls in Tomato Sauce*	1 serving	335
Asparagus	6 stalks	20
Baked Potato	½	25
Cucumber and Onion Salad*	1 serving	12
Coffee or Tea (black or with artificial sweetener)	1 cup	—
	TOTAL	392

TOTAL CALORIES: 1001

BREAKFAST

	Serving	Calories
Orange Juice	¾ cup	85
Poached Egg (use a non-stick pan, no fat)	1	70
Toast	1 slice	75
Butter or Margarine	½ pat	38
Skim Milk	1 cup	88
Coffee or Tea (black or with artificial sweetener)	1 cup	—
	TOTAL	356

LUNCH

	Serving	Calories
Broiled Mackerel	1 piece	75
Lemon Caper Sauce*		—
Boiled Potato	1	50
Butter or Margarine	½ pat	38
Spinach	½ cup	25
Coleslaw*	1 serving	25
Raspberries	½ cup	46
Coffee or Tea (black or with artificial sweetener)	1 cup	—
	TOTAL	259

DINNER

	Serving	Calories
Lamb Curry*	1 serving	228
Cooked Rice	½ cup	90
Tossed Green Salad	1 cup	15
Delight Salad Dressing*	1 tablespoon	3
Spanish Cream*	1 serving	50
Coffee or Tea (black or with artifical sweetener)	1 cup	—
	TOTAL	386

Never rely on anyone else to keep you alive and healthy. Doctors will help, but the primary obligation is yours. You owe it to your family as well as to yourself. Keep your weight to what it ought to be.

TOTAL CALORIES: 1008

BREAKFAST

	Serving	Calories
Cantaloupe	½	45
Scrambled Egg*	1	76
Toast	1 slice	75
Butter or Margarine	½ pat	38
Skim Milk	1 cup	88
Coffee or Tea (black or with artificial sweetener)	1 cup	—
	TOTAL	**322**

LUNCH

Madrilene*	1 cup	50
Tuna Fish Salad*	1 serving	140
Melba Toast	1 slice	16
Butter or Margarine	½ pat	38
Skim Milk	1 cup	88
	TOTAL	**332**

DINNER

Cabbage Soup		
Cooked Cabbage	½ cup	20
Bouillon (use 1 cube)	1 cup	11
Corned Beef (lean)	1 (4″ x 3″ x ⅜″) slice	100
Watercress and Tomato Salad	1 serving	30
Vinegar Dressing*		—
Boiled Potato	1	50
Creole Celery*	1 serving	55
Peaches in Sherry*	1 serving	88
Coffee or Tea (black or with artificial sweetener)	1 cup	—
	TOTAL	**354**

TOTAL CALORIES: 979

BREAKFAST

	Serving	Calories
Orange Juice	½ cup	75
Hot Oatmeal	½ cup	80
Sugar	1 teaspoon	16
Skim Milk	1 cup	88
Toast	1 slice	75
Butter or Margarine	½ pat	38
Coffee or Tea (black or with artificial sweetener)	1 cup	—
	TOTAL	372

LUNCH

Tomato Aspic Salad*	1 serving	30
Cold Shrimp (fresh, cleaned, and boiled)	8	72
Tangy Seafood Cocktail Sauce*		—
Deviled Eggs*	1 serving	75
Fresh Apple (cubed)	1	64
Skim Milk	1 cup	88
	TOTAL	329

DINNER

Pan-Broiled Liver*	1 serving	138
Baked Potato	1	50
Butter or Margarine	½ pat	38
Spinach	½ cup	25
Coleslaw*	1 serving	25
Sliced Radish	1	2
Coffee or Tea (black or with artificial sweetener)	1 cup	—
	TOTAL	278

16

TOTAL CALORIES: 1011

BREAKFAST

	Serving	Calories
Banana	½ medium	45
Shredded Wheat	1 biscuit	85
Sugar	1 teaspoon	16
Skim Milk	1 cup	88
Coffee or Tea (black or with artificial sweetener)	1 cup	—
	TOTAL	**234**

LUNCH

	Serving	Calories
Puffed Spanish Omelet*	1 serving	163
Hearts of Lettuce		10
Russian Dressing*	1½ tablespoons	24
Melba Toast	1 slice	16
Butter or Margarine	½ pat	38
Coffee or Tea (black or with artificial sweetener)	1 cup	—
	TOTAL	**251**

DINNER

	Serving	Calories
Clam-Tomato Cocktail*	1 serving	12
Swiss Steak*	1 serving	204
Baked Potato	1	50
Butter or Margarine	½ pat	38
Lima Beans Superb*	1 serving	120
Strawberries	1 cup	82
Diet Sour Cream*	1 tablespoon	20
Coffee or Tea (black or with artificial sweetener)	1 cup	—
	TOTAL	**526**

TOTAL CALORIES: 1000

BREAKFAST

	Serving	Calories
Orange Juice	¾ cup	85
Scrambled Egg*	1	76
Toast	1 slice	75
Butter or Margarine	½ pat	38
Skim Milk	1 cup	88
Coffee or Tea (black or with artificial sweetener)	1 cup	—
	TOTAL	**362**

LUNCH

Baked Chicken Liver*	1 serving	125
Stuffed Tomato Salad*	1 serving	60
Melba Toast	1 slice	16
Butter or Margarine	½ pat	38
Skim Milk	1 cup	88
	TOTAL	**327**

DINNER

Cucumber Cocktail	1 serving	—
Tangy Barbecue Chicken*	1 serving	235
Baked Potato	1	50
Asparagus	6 stalks	20
Radish Curls	3	6
Coffee Whip*	1 serving	—
Coffee or Tea (black or with artificial sweetener)	1 cup	—
	TOTAL	**311**

18

TOTAL CALORIES: 1019

BREAKFAST

	Serving		Calories
Grapefruit Juice	½ cup		50
Soft-Boiled Egg	1		70
Toast	1 slice		75
Butter or Margarine	½ pat		38
Skim Milk	1 cup		88
Coffee or Tea (black or with artificial sweetener)	1 cup		—
		TOTAL	321

LUNCH

Chunky Gazpacho*	1 serving		50
Liverwurst Sandwich			
Liverwurst	1-ounce slice		85
Rye Bread	1 slice		55
Mustard			—
Skim Milk	1 cup		88
		TOTAL	278

DINNER

Chinese-Style Beef and Vegetables*	1 serving		330
Cooked Rice	½ cup		90
Jasmine Tea	1 cup		—
		TOTAL	420

TOTAL CALORIES: 980

BREAKFAST

	Serving	Calories
Tomato Juice	½ cup	28
Broiled Brook Trout with Lemon and Parsley	1	100
Toast	1 slice	75
Butter or Margarine	½ pat	38
Skim Milk	1 cup	88
Coffee or Tea (black or with artificial sweetener)	1 cup	—
	TOTAL	**329**

LUNCH

Egg Bouillon*	1 cup	75
Baked Chicken Drumstick	1	105
Baked Mashed Squash*	1 serving	80
Beet and Onion Salad*	1 serving	60
Blueberries	½ cup	68
Coffee or Tea (black or with artificial sweetener)	1 cup	—
	TOTAL	**388**

DINNER

Russian Borscht*	1 cup	—
Ovenburgers*	1 serving	165
Hot Potato Salad	1 serving	60
Asparagus	6 stalks	20
Tossed Green Salad	1 cup	15
Delight Salad Dressing*	1 tablespoon	3
Coffee or Tea (black or with artificial sweetener)	1 cup	—
	TOTAL	**263**

TOTAL CALORIES: 1007

BREAKFAST

	Serving	Calories
Broiled Grapefruit* (pink)	1 serving	85
Soft-Boiled Egg	1	70
Toast	1 slice	75
Butter or Margarine	½ pat	38
Skim Milk	1 cup	88
Coffee or Tea (black or with artificial sweetener)	1 cup	—
	TOTAL	356

LUNCH

Fresh Shrimp Cocktail	8 shrimp	72
Tangy Seafood Cocktail Sauce*		—
Melba Toast	1 slice	16
Butter or Margarine	½ pat	38
Orange-Cheese Salad*	1 serving	125
Coffee or Tea (black or with artificial sweetener)	1 cup	—
	TOTAL	251

DINNER

Chicken Florentine*	1 serving	219
Baked Potato	1	50
Diet Sour Cream*	1 tablespoon	20
Tossed Green Salad	1 cup	15
Delight Salad Dressing*	1 tablespoon	3
Double Apricot Souffle*	1 serving	63
Ginger Snap	1	30
Coffee or Tea (black or with artificial sweetener)	1 cup	—
	TOTAL	400

TOTAL CALORIES: 1001

BREAKFAST

	Serving	Calories
Orange Juice	½ cup	75
French Toast (use a non-stick pan, no fat)	1 slice	100
Confectioners' Sugar	1 tablespoon	30
Skim Milk	1 cup	88
Coffee or Tea (black or with		
artificial sweetener)	1 cup	—
	TOTAL	293

LUNCH

	Serving	Calories
Madrilene*	1 cup	50
Chicken Salad*	1 serving	180
Frozen Plum Creme*	1 serving	145
Coffee or Tea (black or with		
artificial sweetener)	1 cup	—
	TOTAL	375

DINNER

	Serving	Calories
Oven Croquettes*	1 serving	165
Oven French Fries*	1 serving	100
Green Beans	½ cup	22
Tossed Green Salad	1 cup	15
Delight Salad Dressing*	1 tablespoon	3
Fresh Apricot	1	28
Coffee or Tea (black or with		
artificial sweetener)	1 cup	—
	TOTAL	333

Keep track of the calories you've resisted—340 calories for the hot fudge sundae you passed up.

TOTAL CALORIES: 1000

BREAKFAST

	Serving	Calories
Pear (canned in syrup)	2 halves	75
Rice Krispies	¾ cup	81
Sugar	1 teaspoon	16
Skim Milk	1 cup	88
Coffee or Tea (black or with artificial sweetener)	1 cup	—
	TOTAL	**260**

LUNCH

Mushroom Soup, Country Style*	1 cup	50
Swiss Luncheon Custard*	1 serving	268
Tossed Green Salad	1 cup	15
Tomato Juice Dressing*	1 tablespoon	—
Coffee or Tea (black or with artificial sweetener)	1 cup	—
	TOTAL	**333**

DINNER

Veal with Herb Sauce*	1 serving	239
Baked Potato	1	50
Butter or Margarine	½ pat	38
Brussel Sprouts	4 sprouts	50
Cherry-Fruit Salad*	1 serving	30
Lemon Sherry Dressing*		—
Coffee or Tea (black or with artificial sweetener)	1 cup	—
	TOTAL	**407**

TOTAL CALORIES: 1000

BREAKFAST

	Serving	Calories
Pineapple Juice (canned)	½ cup	54
Soft-Boiled Egg	1	70
Toast	1 slice	75
Butter or Margarine	½ pat	38
Skim Milk	1 cup	88
Coffee or Tea (black or with artificial sweetener)	1 cup	—
	TOTAL	325

LUNCH

Chunky Gazpacho*	1 serving	50
Veal and Mushroom Aspic*	1 serving	75
Asparagus and Pimiento Salad*	1 serving	12
Ry-Krisp (seasoned and toasted)	2 triple crackers	50
Fresh Tangerine	1	50
Skim Milk	1 cup	88
	TOTAL	325

DINNER

Braised Beef Roll-Ups*	1 serving	260
Barbecue Dressing*		—
Baked Potato	1	50
Spinach	½ cup	25
Tossed Green Salad	1 cup	15
Vinegar Dressing*		—
Coffee Whip*	1 serving	—
Coffee or Tea (black or with artificial sweetener)	1 cup	—
	TOTAL	350

TOTAL CALORIES: 992

BREAKFAST

	Serving	Calories
Tomato Juice	½ cup	28
Hot Oatmeal	½ cup	80
Sugar	1 teaspoon	16
Skim Milk	1 cup	88
Coffee or Tea (black or with artificial sweetener)	1 cup	—
	TOTAL	212

LUNCH

Tuna Fish Salad*	1 serving	140
Deviled Eggs*	2 halves	75
Melba Toast	1 slice	16
Butter or Margarine	½ pat	38
Strawberries	½ cup	41
Diet Sour Cream*	1 teaspoon	10
Coffee or Tea (black or with artificial sweetener)	1 cup	—
	TOTAL	320

DINNER

Chicken Pot Pie*	1 serving	335
Baked Potato	1	50
Tossed Green Salad	1 cup	15
Sliced Tomato	½	15
Vinegar Dressing*		—
Cantaloupe	½	45
Coffee or Tea (black or with artificial sweetener)	1 cup	—
	TOTAL	460

TOTAL CALORIES: 1006

BREAKFAST

	Serving	Calories
Orange Juice	¾ cup	85
Poached Egg (use a non-stick pan, no fat)	1	70
Toast	1 slice	75
Butter or Margarine	½ pat	38
Skim Milk	1 cup	88
Coffee or Tea (black or with artificial sweetener)	1 cup	—
	TOTAL	**356**

LUNCH

	Serving	Calories
Fruit Platter with Cheese*	1 serving	190
No-Calorie Fruit Dressing*		—
Melba Toast	1 slice	16
Skim Milk Custard*	1 serving	135
Coffee or Tea (black or with artificial sweetener)	1 cup	—
	TOTAL	**341**

DINNER

	Serving	Calories
Roast Turkey	1 (4" x 2½" x ¼") slice	100
Cranberry-Orange Relish*		—
Mashed Potato	½ cup	85
Butter or Margarine	½ pat	38
Cooked Cauliflower	½ cup	31
Endive and Pepper Salad*	1 serving	55
Coffee or Tea (black or with artificial sweetener)	1 cup	—
	TOTAL	**309**

27

TOTAL CALORIES: 1010

BREAKFAST

	Serving	Calories
Cantaloupe	½	45
Poached Egg Supreme*	1	205
Skim Milk	1 cup	88
Coffee or Tea (black or with artificial sweetener)	1 cup	—
	TOTAL	**338**

LUNCH

	Serving	Calories
Boiled Ham Sandwich		
Boiled Ham	1 slice	100
Lettuce	2 leaves	6
Tomato	1	17
Bread	2 (¼"-thick) slices	75
Orange	1	50
Skim Milk	1 cup	88
	TOTAL	**336**

DINNER

	Serving	Calories
Tomato-Celery Soup*	1 cup	—
Sweet and Sour Shrimp*	1 serving	200
Steamed Rice	¾ cup	102
Cucumber and Onion Salad*	1 serving	12
Green Beans	½ cup	22
Coffee or Tea (black or with artificial sweetener)	1 cup	—
	TOTAL	**336**

28

TOTAL CALORIES: 1005

BREAKFAST

	Serving	Calories
Pineapple Juice (canned)	½ cup	54
Poached Egg (use a non-stick pan, no fat)	1	70
Toast	1 slice	75
Butter or Margarine	½ pat	38
Skim Milk	1 cup	88
Coffee or Tea (black or with artificial sweetener)	1 cup	—
	TOTAL	325

LUNCH

Salad Soup*	1 cup	12
Skewer of Chicken Livers and Tomato*	1 skewer	150
Peas (canned)	½ cup	69
Coleslaw*	1 serving	25
Skim Milk	1 cup	88
Coffee or Tea (black or with artificial sweetener)	1 cup	—
	TOTAL	344

DINNER

Swiss Steak*	1 serving	204
Boiled Potato	1	50
Butter or Margarine	½ pat	38
Carrots and Mushrooms*	1 serving	35
Stewed Rhubarb (with artificial sweetener)	¼ cup	9
Coffee or Tea (black or with artificial sweetener)	1 cup	—
	TOTAL	336

29

TOTAL CALORIES: 1015

BREAKFAST

	Serving		Calories
Blueberries	½ cup		68
Scrambled Egg*	1		76
Toast	1 slice		75
Butter or Margarine	½ pat		38
Skim Milk	1 cup		88
Coffee or Tea (black or with artificial sweetener)	1 cup		—
		TOTAL	345

LUNCH

	Serving		Calories
Clam-Tomato Cocktail*	1 serving		12
Cottage Cheese	½ cup		120
Asparagus and Pimiento Salad*	1 serving		12
Raw Carrots, shredded	½ cup		25
Skim Milk Custard*	1 serving		135
		TOTAL	304

DINNER

	Serving		Calories
Fillet of Sole Veronique*	1 serving		291
Baked Potato	1		50
Spinach	½ cup		25
Lemon Gelatin*	1 serving		—
Coffee or Tea (black or with artificial sweetener)	1 cup		—
		TOTAL	366

TOTAL CALORIES: 1003

BREAKFAST

	Serving	Calories
Tomato Juice	½ cup	28
Soft-Boiled Egg	1	70
Pork Sausage	1 link	70
Toast	1 slice	75
Butter or Margarine	½ pat	38
Coffee or Tea (black or with artificial sweetener)	1 cup	—
	TOTAL	**281**

LUNCH

Fruit Platter with Cheese*	1 serving	190
Italian Bread Stick	1 long	39
Skim Milk	1 cup	88
	TOTAL	**317**

DINNER

Broiled Sirloin Steak*	¼ pound	238
Baked Potato	1	50
Diet Sour Cream*	1 tablespoon	20
Beet and Onion Salad*	1 serving	60
Broccoli	½ cup	37
Coffee or Tea (black or with artificial sweetener)	1 cup	—
	TOTAL	**405**

TOTAL CALORIES: 999

BREAKFAST

	Serving	Calories
Fresh Pineapple	1"-thick slice	50
Poached Egg (use a non-stick pan, no fat)	1	70
Toast	1 slice	75
Butter or Margarine	½ pat	38
Skim Milk	1 cup	88
Coffee or Tea (black or with artificial sweetener)	1 cup	—
	TOTAL	321

LUNCH

Broiled Frankfurter	1	115
Sauerkraut	½ cup	20
Dieter's Potato Salad*	1 serving	100
Raw Carrots, shredded	½ cup	25
Lime-Melon Mold*	1 serving	25
Iced Tea	1 glass	—
	TOTAL	285

DINNER

Minted Buttermilk Soup*	1 cup	85
Flounder and Horseradish Sauce*	1 serving	125
Parsley Potatoes	1	50
Butter or Margarine	½ pat	38
Lemon-Chive Asparagus Spears*	1 serving	70
Grape Gelatin*	1 serving	25
Coffee or Tea (black or with artificial sweetener)	1 cup	—
	TOTAL	393

TOTAL CALORIES: 997

BREAKFAST

	Serving	Calories
Grapefruit	½ medium	60
Scrambled Egg*	1	76
Toast	1 slice	75
Butter or Margarine	½ pat	38
Skim Milk	1 cup	88
Coffee or Tea (black or with artificial sweetener)	1 cup	—
	TOTAL	337

LUNCH

Baked Chicken Livers*	1 serving	125
Rice	½ cup	90
Stuffed Tomato Salad*	1 serving	60
Lime-Melon Mold*	1 serving	25
Coffee or Tea (black or with artificial sweetener)	1 cup	—
	TOTAL	300

DINNER

Mushroom Soup, Country Style*	1 cup	50
Beef Patties Burgundy*	1 serving	180
Parsley Carrots and Potatoes*	1 serving	105
Coleslaw*	1 serving	25
Coffee or Tea (black or with artificial sweetener)	1 cup	—
	TOTAL	360

TOTAL CALORIES: 998

BREAKFAST

	Serving	Calories
Fresh Pear	1	70
Soft-Boiled Egg	1	70
Toast	1 slice	75
Butter or Margarine	½ pat	38
Skim Milk	1 cup	88
Coffee or Tea (black or with artificial sweetener)	1 cup	—
	TOTAL	**341**

LUNCH

	Serving	Calories
Tomato Juice	½ cup	28
Broiled Open-face Roast Beef Sandwich		
Roast Beef	3 ounces lean meat	175
Rye Bread	1 slice	55
Hearts of Lettuce	1 cup	9
Vinegar Dressing*		—
Skim Milk	1 cup	88
	TOTAL	**355**

DINNER

	Serving	Calories
Broiled Lamb Chop	1	100
Parsley Rice*	1 serving	140
Green Beans	½ cup	22
Tossed Green Salad	1 cup	15
Sliced Tomato	½	15
Vinegar Dressing*		—
Raw Celery	3 small inner stalks	10
Coffee or Tea (black or with artificial sweetener)	1 cup	—
	TOTAL	**302**

34

TOTAL CALORIES: 1001

BREAKFAST

	Serving	Calories
Carrot Juice	½ cup	50
Soft-Boiled Egg	1	70
Toast	1 slice	75
Butter or Margarine	½ pat	38
Skim Milk	1 cup	88
Coffee or Tea (black or with artificial sweetener)	1 cup	—
	TOTAL	**321**

LUNCH

	Serving	Calories
Crabmeat Salad*	1 serving	100
Ry-Krisp (seasoned and toasted)	2 triple crackers	50
Skim Milk Custard*	1 serving	135
Coffee or Tea (black or with artificial sweetener)	1 cup	—
	TOTAL	**285**

DINNER

	Serving	Calories
Spiced Veal Cutlet*	1 serving	230
Baked Potato	1	50
Butter or Margarine	½ pat	38
Green Beans	½ cup	22
Tossed Green Salad	1 cup	15
Tomato Juice Dressing*		—
Apricot Fluff*	1 serving	40
Coffee or Tea (black or with artificial sweetener)	1 cup	—
	TOTAL	**395**

35

TOTAL CALORIES: 1001

BREAKFAST

	Serving	Calories
Tomato Juice	1 cup	50
French Toast (use a non-stick pan, no fat)	1 slice	100
Confectioners' Sugar	1 teaspoon	21
Skim Milk	1 cup	88
Coffee or Tea (black or with artificial sweetener)	1 cup	—
	TOTAL	**259**

LUNCH

	Serving	Calories
Mushroom Soup, Country Style*	1 cup	50
Broiled Open-face Roast Beef Sandwich		
Roast Beef (lean)	3 ounces	175
Rye Bread	1 slice	55
Hearts of Lettuce		10
Russian Dressing*	1½ teaspoons	24
Spanish Cream*	1 serving	50
	TOTAL	**364**

DINNER

	Serving	Calories
Broiled Halibut Steak	1 (3" x 1¼" x 1") slice	100
Lemon Caper Sauce*		—
Baked Potato	1	50
Butter or Margarine	½ pat	38
Savory Green Beans*	1 serving	65
Orange-Cheese Salad*	1 serving	125
Coffee or Tea (black or with artificial sweetener)	1 cup	—
	TOTAL	**378**

TOTAL CALORIES: 1004

BREAKFAST

	Serving	Calories
Grapefruit Juice	½ cup	50
Poached Egg (use a non-stick pan, no fat)	1	70
Toast	1 slice	75
Butter or Margarine	½ pat	38
Skim Milk	1 cup	88
Coffee or Tea (black or with artificial sweetener)	1 cup	—
	TOTAL	**321**

LUNCH

Pan-Broiled Liver*	1 serving	138
Mixed Vegetable Salad*	1 serving	15
Peaches in Sherry*	1 serving	88
Skim Milk	1 cup	88
	TOTAL	**329**

DINNER

Broiled Fillet of Bass	1 piece	50
Lemon-Caper Sauce*		—
Baked Potato	1	50
Butter or Margarine	½ pat	38
Spinach	½ cup	25
Citrus Salad*	1 serving	90
Orange-Tapioca Pudding	1 serving	85
Lemon Snap	1	16
Coffee or Tea (black or with artificial sweetener)	1 cup	—
	TOTAL	**354**

Tie a bell on your refrigerator door. It will provide a musical reminder of the potential diet-wreckers lurking inside.

TOTAL CALORIES: 1009

BREAKFAST

	Serving	Calories
Apple Juice	½ cup	60
Hot Oatmeal	½ cup	80
Sugar	1 teaspoon	16
Skim Milk	1 cup	88
Coffee or Tea (black or with artificial sweetener)	1 cup	—
	TOTAL	244

LUNCH

Egg and Shrimp Salad*	1 serving	175
Tangy Seafood Cocktail Sauce*		—
Melba Toast	1 slice	16
Butter or Margarine	½ pat	38
Fresh Strawberries	½ cup	41
Skim Milk	1 cup	88
	TOTAL	358

DINNER

Veal with Herb Sauce*	1 serving	239
Baked Potato	1	50
Diet Sour Cream* and Chopped Chives	1 teaspoon	10
Broiled Tomato	1	30
Tossed Green Salad	1 cup	15
Tomato Juice Dressing*		—
Double Apricot Souffle*	1 serving	63
Coffee or Tea (black or with artificial sweetener)	1 cup	—
	TOTAL	407

TOTAL CALORIES: 1000

BREAKFAST

	Serving	Calories
Orange Juice	½ cup	75
Hot Oatmeal	½ cup	80
Sugar	1 teaspoon	16
Skim Milk	1 cup	88
Toast	1 slice	75
Butter or Margarine	½ pat	38
Coffee or Tea (black or with artificial sweetener)	1 cup	—
	TOTAL	372

LUNCH

Puffed Spanish Omelet*	1 serving	163
Melba Toast	1 slice	16
Asparagus and Pimiento Salad*	1 serving	12
Cantaloupe	½	45
Skim Milk	1 cup	88
	TOTAL	324

DINNER

Chicken Florentine*	1 serving	219
Baked Potato	1	50
Diet Sour Cream*	1 tablespoon	20
Tossed Green Salad	1 cup	15
Vinegar Dressing*		—
Coffee Whip*	1 serving	—
	TOTAL	304

TOTAL CALORIES: 990

BREAKFAST

	Serving	Calories
Apple Juice	½ cup	60
Soft-Boiled Egg	1	70
Toast	1 slice	75
Butter or Margarine	½ pat	38
Skim Milk	1 cup	88
Coffee or Tea (black or with artificial sweetener)	1 cup	—
	TOTAL	331

LUNCH

	Serving	Calories
Chicken Salad*	1 serving	180
Melba Toast	1 slice	16
Butter or Margarine	½ pat	38
Strawberries	½ cup	41
Diet Sour Cream*	1 tablespoon	20
Skim Milk	1 cup	88
Coffee or Tea (black or with artificial sweetener)	1 cup	—
	TOTAL	383

DINNER

	Serving	Calories
Baked Codfish with Grapefruit*	1 serving	140
Baked Acorn Squash*	1 serving	75
Coleslaw*	1 serving	25
Asparagus	6 stalks	20
Lemon Snap	1	16
Coffee or Tea (black or with artificial sweetener)	1 cup	—
	TOTAL	276

TOTAL CALORIES: 993

BREAKFAST

	Serving	Calories
Tomato Juice	1 cup	50
Soft-Boiled Egg	1	70
Toast	1 slice	75
Butter or Margarine	½ pat	38
Skim Milk	1 cup	88
Coffee or Tea (black or with artificial sweetener)	1 cup	—
	TOTAL	321

LUNCH

	Serving	Calories
Hearty Vegetable Soup*	1 cup	95
Ry-Krisp (seasoned and toasted)	1 triple cracker	25
Butter or Margarine	½ pat	38
Watercress and Tomato Salad		
Watercress	1 cup	15
Sliced Tomato	½	8
Delight Salad Dressing*	1 tablespoon	3
Uncreamed Cottage Cheese	2 tablespoons	25
Coffee or Tea (black or with artificial sweetener)	1 cup	—
	TOTAL	209

DINNER

	Serving	Calories
Golden Peachy Chicken*	1 serving	205
Baked Potato	1	50
Diet Sour Cream*	1 tablespoon	20
Southern Green Beans*	1 serving	65
Tossed Green Salad	1 cup	15
Chopped Celery	¼ cup	5
Sliced Cucumber	½	15
Vinegar Dressing*		—
Skim Milk	1 cup	88
	TOTAL	463

TOTAL CALORIES: 999

BREAKFAST

	Serving	Calories
Tomato Juice	½ cup	28
Soft-Boiled Egg	1	70
Toast	1 slice	75
Butter or Margarine	½ pat	38
Skim Milk	1 cup	88
Coffee or Tea (black or with artificial sweetener)	1 cup	—
	TOTAL	299

LUNCH

Minted Buttermilk Soup*	1 cup	85
Skewer of Chicken Livers and Tomato*	1 skewer	150
Spinach	½ cup	25
Beet and Onion Salad*	1 serving	60
Coffee or Tea (black or with artificial sweetener)	1 cup	—
	TOTAL	320

DINNER

Fillet of Sole Valenciennes*	1 serving	150
Scalloped Potatoes*	1 serving	125
Parsley Carrots and Potatoes*	1 serving	105
Lemon Gelatin*	1 serving	—
Coffee or Tea (black or with artificial sweetener)	1 cup	—
	TOTAL	380

TOTAL CALORIES: 996

BREAKFAST

	Serving	Calories
Grapefruit	½	44
Bacon (thin)	1 strip	30
Toast	1 slice	75
Butter or Margarine	½ pat	38
Skim Milk	1 cup	88
Coffee or Tea (black or with artificial sweetener)	1 cup	—
	TOTAL	275

LUNCH

Egg Bouillon*	1 cup	75
Crabmeat Salad*	1 serving	100
Ry-Krisp (seasoned and toasted)	1 triple cracker	25
Apricot (canned in syrup)	2 halves	60
Skim Milk	1 cup	88
	TOTAL	348

DINNER

Stuffed Green Peppers*	1 serving	250
Baked Potato	1	50
Butter or Margarine	½ pat	38
Asparagus	6 stalks	20
Tossed Green Salad	1 cup	15
Tomato Juice Dressing*		—
Coffee or Tea (black or with artificial sweetener)	1 cup	—
	TOTAL	373

TOTAL CALORIES: 993

BREAKFAST

	Serving	Calories
Cantaloupe	½	45
Bacon (thin and crisp)	1 strip	30
English Muffin	½	70
Butter or Margarine	½ pat	38
Citrus Marmalade	1 teaspoon	25
Skim Milk	1 cup	88
Coffee or Tea (black or with artificial sweetener)	1 cup	—
	TOTAL	296

LUNCH

	Serving	Calories
Omelet with Fine Herbs*	1 serving	200
Watercress and Tomato Salad	1 serving	23
Vinegar Dressing*		—
Coffee or Tea (black or with artificial sweetener)	1 cup	—
	TOTAL	223

DINNER

	Serving	Calories
Bouillon (use 1 cube)	1 cup	11
Fillet of Sole Veronique*	1 serving	291
Parsley Potato	1	50
Cooked Carrots	½ cup	25
Asparagus and Pimiento Salad*	1 serving	12
Broiled Grapefruit*	½	85
Coffee or Tea (black or with artificial sweetener)	1 cup	—
	TOTAL	474

45

TOTAL CALORIES: 1008

BREAKFAST

	Serving		Calories
Fresh Apple (peeled and diced)	1		64
Hot Cereal	¾ cup		100
Sugar	1 teaspoon		16
Skim Milk	1 cup		88
Coffee or Tea (black or with artificial sweetener)	1 cup		—
		TOTAL	268

LUNCH

Egg Bouillon*	1 cup		75
Veal and Mushroom Aspic*	1 serving		75
Sliced Tomato and Watercress	1 serving		35
Melba Toast	1 slice		16
Butter or Margarine	½ pat		38
Coffee or Tea (black or with artificial sweetener)	1 cup		—
		TOTAL	239

DINNER

Tomato Juice	1 cup		50
Fillet of Sole Valenciennes*	1 serving		150
Baked Potato	1		50
Curried Mixed Vegetables*	1 serving		65
Lime-Cabbage Salad*	1 serving		80
Stewed Rhubarb (with artificial sweetener)	½ cup		18
Skim Milk	1 cup		88
Coffee or Tea (black or with artificial sweetener)	1 cup		—
		TOTAL	501

When using butter or margarine, let your food cool slightly before you apply it. The hotter a baked potato is, the more butter it drinks up.

TOTAL CALORIES: 1005

BREAKFAST

	Serving		Calories
Orange Juice	¾ cup		85
Soft-Boiled Egg	1		70
Toast	1 slice		75
Butter or Margarine	½ pat		38
Skim Milk	1 cup		88
Coffee or Tea (black or with artificial sweetener)	1 cup		—
		TOTAL	356

LUNCH

	Serving		Calories
Chicken Jambalaya*	1 serving		250
Tossed Green Salad	1 cup		15
Vinegar Dressing*			—
Melba Toast	1 slice		16
Skim Milk	1 cup		88
		TOTAL	369

DINNER

	Serving		Calories
Fruit Cocktail (canned in syrup)	½ cup		78
Roast Leg of Lamb	1 slice		100
Green Beans	½ cup		22
Parsley Potato	1		50
Tomato Aspic Salad*	1 serving		30
Coffee or Tea (black or with artificial sweetener)	1 cup		—
		TOTAL	280

TOTAL CALORIES: 1000

BREAKFAST

	Serving	Calories
Grapefruit	½	44
Bacon (thin)	1 strip	30
Toast	1 slice	75
Butter or Margarine	½ pat	38
Skim Milk	1 cup	88
Coffee or Tea (black or with artificial sweetener)	1 cup	—
	TOTAL	275

LUNCH

Swiss Luncheon Custard*	1 serving	268
Savory Green Beans*	1 serving	65
Cucumber and Onion Salad*	1 serving	12
Coffee or Tea (black or with artificial sweetener)	1 cup	—
	TOTAL	345

DINNER

Sweet and Sour Shrimp*	1 serving	200
Rice	½ cup	90
Cooked Kale	½ cup	30
Spring Garden Salad*	1 serving	60
Coffee or Tea (black or with artificial sweetener)	1 cup	—
	TOTAL	380

TOTAL CALORIES: 1000

BREAKFAST

	Serving	Calories
Blueberries	½ cup	68
Scrambled Egg*	1	78
Toast	1 slice	75
Butter or Margarine	½ pat	38
Skim Milk	1 cup	88
Coffee or Tea (black or with artificial sweetener)	1 cup	—
	TOTAL	347

LUNCH

	Serving	Calories
Salmon Salad	½ cup	135
Ry-Krisp (seasoned and toasted)	2 triple crackers	50
Butter or Margarine	½ pat	38
Skim Milk Custard*	1 serving	135
Coffee or Tea (black or with artificial sweetener)	1 cup	—
	TOTAL	358

DINNER

	Serving	Calories
Clam-Tomato Cocktail*	1 serving	12
Baked Chicken Livers*	1 serving	125
Baked Potato	1	50
Diet Sour Cream*	1 tablespoon	20
Green Beans	½ cup	22
Spring Garden Salad*	1 serving	60
Raw Celery	2 small inner stalks	6
Coffee or Tea (black or with artificial sweetener)	1 cup	—
	TOTAL	295

TOTAL CALORIES: 999

BREAKFAST

	Serving		Calories
Tomato Juice	½ cup		28
Soft-Boiled Egg	1		70
Toast	1 slice		75
Butter or Margarine	½ pat		38
Skim Milk	1 cup		88
Coffee or Tea (black or with artificial sweetener)	1 cup		—
		TOTAL	299

LUNCH

Creole Shrimp*	1 serving		360
Cooked Rice	½ cup		90
Tossed Green Salad	1 cup		15
Vinegar Dressing*			—
Coffee or Tea (black or with artificial sweetener)	1 cup		—
		TOTAL	465

DINNER

Russian Borscht*	1 cup		—
Skewer of Chicken Livers and Tomato*	1 skewer		150
Hot Potato Salad*	1 serving		60
Boiled Cabbage	1 cup		25
Coffee or Tea (black or with artificial sweetener)	1 cup		—
		TOTAL	235

TOTAL CALORIES: 1005

BREAKFAST

	Serving	Calories
Apple Juice	½ cup	60
Puffed Wheat	1 cup	45
Sugar	1 teaspoon	16
Skim Milk	1 cup	88
Coffee or Tea		
(black or with		
artificial sweetener)	1 cup	—
	TOTAL	**209**

LUNCH

Tomato Aspic Salad*	1 serving	30
Grilled Cube Steak (½ teaspoon fat)	3½ ounces	210
on toast	1 slice	75
Hot Potato Salad*	1 serving	60
Iced Tea	1 glass	—
	TOTAL	**375**

DINNER

Crabmeat Orange Crepes*	1 serving	234
Broccoli	½ cup	37
Mixed Green Salad	1 cup	15
Vinegar Dressing*		—
Skim Milk Custard*	1 serving	135
Coffee or Tea (black or with		
artificial sweetener)	1 cup	—
	TOTAL	**421**

TOTAL CALORIES: 1003

BREAKFAST

	Serving	Calories
Tomato Juice	1 cup	50
French Toast (use a non-stick pan, no fat)	1 slice	100
Confectioners' Sugar	1 teaspoon	21
Skim Milk	1 cup	88
Coffee or Tea (black or with		
artificial sweetener)	1 cup	—
	TOTAL	259

LUNCH

Chicken Gumbo Soup*	1 serving	25
Grilled Cheese Sandwich		
American Processed Cheese	1 ounce	90
Rye Bread	1 slice	55
Skim Milk	1 cup	88
	TOTAL	258

DINNER

Broiled Mackerel	2 pieces	150
Lemon Caper Sauce*		—
Scalloped Potatoes*	1 serving	125
Peas Superb*	1 serving	110
Tossed Green Salad	1 cup	15
Tomato Juice Dressing*		—
Cherries (canned in syrup)	½ cup	86
Coffee or Tea (black or with		
artificial sweetener)	1 cup	—
	TOTAL	486

Once you've arrived at your desired weight
and decide to have a drink at a cocktail party,
watch out for extra calories. Club soda has
virtually no calories but 6 ounces of tonic has
71. Even tomato juice for a Bloody Mary has
40 calories. Stretch your drinks. Pour them long,
tall and mild, then sip slowly. Beware the
maraschino cherry and olive; use a twist of
lemon peel instead.

TOTAL CALORIES: 1009

BREAKFAST

	Serving	Calories
Grapefruit Juice	½ cup	50
Soft-Boiled Egg	1	70
Toast	1 slice	75
Butter or Margarine	½ pat	38
Skim Milk	1 cup	88
Coffee or Tea (black or with artificial sweetener)	1 cup	—
	TOTAL	**321**

LUNCH

	Serving	Calories
Bologna	1 slice	25
American Cheese	1 slice	50
Cottage Cheese	¼ cup	60
Chunky Gazpacho*	1 serving	50
Melba Toast	1 slice	16
Butter or Margarine	½ pat	38
Skim Milk	1 cup	88
	TOTAL	**327**

DINNER

	Serving	Calories
Russian Borscht*	1 cup	—
Diet Sour Cream*	1 teaspoon	10
Dieter's Beef Stroganoff*	1 serving	240
Cooked Rice	¾ cup	102
Quartered Lettuce	1 cup	9
Vinegar Dressing*		—
Coffee or Tea (black or with artificial sweetener)	1 cup	—
	TOTAL	**361**

TOTAL CALORIES: 995

BREAKFAST

	Serving	Calories
Orange Juice	¾ cup	85
Scrambled Egg*	1	76
Toast	1 slice	75
Butter or Margarine	½ pat	38
Skim Milk	1 cup	88
Coffee or Tea (black or with artificial sweetener)	1 cup	—
	TOTAL	**362**

LUNCH

	Serving	Calories
Bouillon (use 1 cube)	1 cup	11
Cottage Cheese and Fruit		
Uncreamed Cottage Cheese	½ cup	110
Sliced Fresh Peaches	½ cup	40
Roll	1 small	85
Butter or Margarine	½ pat	38
Iced Tea with Lemon and Mint	1 glass	—
	TOTAL	**284**

DINNER

	Serving	Calories
Pan-Broiled Liver*	1 (3½″ x 2½″ ⅜″) slice	138
Parsley Potato	1	50
Peas	½ cup	55
Mixed Green Salad	1 cup	15
Delight Salad Dressing*	1 tablespoon	3
Skim Milk	1 cup	88
Coffee or Tea (black or with artificial sweetener)	1 cup	—
	TOTAL	**349**

TOTAL CALORIES: 1025

BREAKFAST

	Serving	Calories
Grapefruit	½ medium	60
Scrambled Egg*	1	76
Toast	1 slice	75
Butter or Margarine	½ pat	38
Coffee or Tea (black or with artificial sweetener)	1 cup	—
	TOTAL	249

LUNCH

Hot Vegetable Soup	1 cup	70
Swiss Cheese Sandwich		
Cheese	1 ounce	105
Mustard		—
Rye Bread	1 slice	55
Skim Milk	1 cup	88
	TOTAL	318

DINNER

Roast Beef (sirloin—lean meat only)	¼ pound	235
Baked Acorn Squash*	½ squash	75
Brussels Sprouts with Mushrooms	½ cup	30
Tomato Aspic* on Chicory	1 serving	30
Skim Milk	1 cup	88
Coffee or Tea (black or with artificial sweetener)	1 cup	—
	TOTAL	458

TOTAL CALORIES: 1012

BREAKFAST

	Serving	Calories
Tomato Juice	1 cup	**50**
French Toast (use a non-stick pan, no fat)	1 slice	**100**
Confectioners' Sugar	1 teaspoon	**21**
Skim Milk	1 cup	**88**
Coffee or Tea (black or with		
artificial sweetener)	1 cup	**—**
	TOTAL	**259**

LUNCH

	Serving	Calories
Shrimp Salad		
Shrimp	3 ounces	**110**
Celery	¼ cup	**5**
Dieter's Mayonnaise*	1 tablespoon	**15**
Lettuce	2 leaves	**—**
Melba Toast	1 slice	**16**
Butter or Margarine	½ pat	**38**
Skim Milk	1 cup	**88**
	TOTAL	**272**

DINNER

	Serving	Calories
Oven Croquettes*	2	**165**
Baked Potato	1	**50**
Butter or Margarine	½ pat	**38**
Herbed Lima Beans*	1 serving	**120**
Lime-Cabbage Salad*	1 serving	**80**
Fresh Apricot	1	**28**
Coffee or Tea (black or with		
artificial sweetener)	1 cup	**—**
	TOTAL	**481**

TOTAL CALORIES: 1000

BREAKFAST

	Serving	Calories
Grapefruit	½	44
Bacon (thin)	1 strip	30
Toast	1 slice	75
Butter or Margarine	½ pat	38
Skim Milk	1 cup	88
Coffee or Tea (black or with artificial sweetener)	1 cup	—
	TOTAL	275

LUNCH

Swiss Luncheon Custard*	1 serving	268
Savory Green Beans*	1 serving	65
Cucumber and Onion Salad*	1 serving	12
Coffee or Tea (black or with artificial sweetener)	1 cup	—
	TOTAL	345

DINNER

Sweet and Sour Shrimp*	1 serving	200
Rice	½ cup	90
Cooked Kale	½ cup	30
Spring Garden Salad*	1 serving	60
Coffee or Tea (black or with artificial sweetener)	1 cup	—
	TOTAL	380

59

TOTAL CALORIES: 1004

BREAKFAST

	Serving	Calories
Grapefruit Juice	½ cup	50
Poached Egg (use a non-stick pan, no fat)	1	70
Toast	1 slice	75
Butter or Margarine	½ pat	38
Skim Milk	1 cup	88
Coffee or Tea (black or with artificial sweetener)	1 cup	—
	TOTAL	**321**

LUNCH

Pan-Broiled Liver*	1 serving	138
Mixed Vegetable Salad*	1 serving	15
Peaches in Sherry*	1 serving	88
Skim Milk	1 cup	88
	TOTAL	**329**

DINNER

Broiled Fillet of Bass	1 piece	50
Lemon-Caper Sauce*		—
Baked Potato	1	50
Butter or Margarine	½ pat	38
Spinach	½ cup	25
Citrus Salad*	1 serving	90
Orange-Tapioca Pudding*	1 serving	85
Lemon Snap	1	16
Coffee or Tea (black or with artificial sweetener)	1 cup	—
	TOTAL	**354**

TOTAL CALORIES: 1017

BREAKFAST

	Serving	Calories
Cantaloupe	½ medium	40
Broiled Brook Trout with Lemon and Parsley	1 piece	100
Toast	1 piece	75
Butter or Margarine	½ pat	38
Skim Milk	1 cup	88
Coffee or Tea (black or with artificial sweetener)	1 cup	—
	TOTAL	341

LUNCH

Tomato Juice	1 cup	50
Omelet with Fine Herbs*	1 serving	200
Melba Toast	1 slice	16
Cooked Spinach with Lemon	½ cup	25
Skim Milk	1 cup	88
	TOTAL	379

DINNER

Ovenburgers*	1 serving	165
Parsley Potato	1	50
Creole Celery*	1 serving	55
Coleslaw*	½ cup	27
Coffee or Tea (black or with artificial sweetener)	1 cup	—
	TOTAL	297

TOTAL CALORIES: 994

BREAKFAST

	Serving	Calories
Fresh Grapefruit Sections	½ cup	40
Hot Oatmeal	½ cup	80
Sugar	1 teaspoon	16
Skim Milk	½ cup	44
Toast	1 slice	75
Butter or Margarine	½ pat	38
Coffee or Tea (black or with artificial sweetener)	1 cup	—
	TOTAL	293

LUNCH

Omelet	1 egg	125
Rye Toast	2 slices	110
Butter or Margarine	½ pat	38
Cherry Fruit Salad*	1 serving	30
Skim Milk	1 cup	88
	TOTAL	391

DINNER

Baked Ham (lean)	3 ounces	160
Cooked Kale	½ cup	30
Baked Potato	1	50
Spring Garden Salad*	1 serving	60
Red Button Radishes	5	10
Coffee or Tea (black or with artificial sweetener)	1 cup	—
	TOTAL	310

TOTAL CALORIES: 1034

BREAKFAST

	Serving	Calories
Applesauce (unsweetened)	½ cup	50
Scrambled Egg*	1	76
Toast	1 slice	75
Butter or Margarine	½ pat	38
Skim Milk	1 cup	88
Coffee or Tea (black or with artificial sweetener)	1 cup	—
	TOTAL	327

LUNCH

	Serving	Calories
Tomato Soup (plain)	½ cup	46
Pan-Broiled Liver*	1 serving	138
Hot Potato Salad*	1 serving	60
Savory Green Beans*	1 serving	65
Skim Milk	1 cup	88
	TOTAL	397

DINNER

	Serving	Calories
Beef Patties Burgundy*	1 serving	180
Broccoli with Mustard Dill Sauce*	1 serving	80
Spinach and Radish Salad*	1 serving	50
Coffee or Tea (black or with artificial sweetener)	1 cup	—
	TOTAL	310

TOTAL CALORIES: 1005

BREAKFAST

	Serving	Calories
Apple Juice	½ cup	60
Scrambled Egg*	1	76
Toast	1 slice	75
Butter or Margarine	½ pat	38
Skim Milk	1 cup	88
Coffee or Tea (black or with artificial sweetener)	1 cup	—
	TOTAL	337

LUNCH

	Serving	Calories
Salmon Baked in Foil*	1 serving	315
Parsley Potato	1	50
Butter or Margarine	½ pat	38
Spinach	½ cup	25
Iced Tea with Lemon	1 glass	—
	TOTAL	428

DINNER

	Serving	Calories
Tomato-Celery Soup*	1 cup	—
Stuffed Tomato Salad*	1 serving	60
Skewered Lamb with Pineapple*	1 skewer	180
Lemon Gelatin*	1 serving	—
	TOTAL	240

TOTAL CALORIES: 1016

BREAKFAST

	Serving	Calories
Cantaloupe	½	45
Poached Egg Supreme*	1	205
Skim Milk	1 cup	88
Coffee or Tea (black or with artificial sweetener)	1 cup	—
	TOTAL	338

LUNCH

	Serving	Calories
Cream of Tomato Soup (made with skim milk)	1 cup	105
Chicken Salad*	1 serving	180
Rye Bread	1 slice	55
Butter or Margarine	½ pat	38
Iced Tea with Lemon	1 glass	—
	TOTAL	378

DINNER

	Serving	Calories
Fish Pie	1 serving	280
Asparagus	6 stalks	20
Coffee Whip*	1 serving	—
Coffee or Tea (black or with artificial sweetener)	1 cup	—
	TOTAL	300

TOTAL CALORIES: 1013

BREAKFAST

	Serving	Calories
Orange Juice	¾ cup	85
Scrambled Egg*	1	76
Toast	1 slice	75
Butter or Margarine	½ pat	38
Skim Milk	1 cup	88
Coffee or Tea (black or with artificial sweetener)	1 cup	—
	TOTAL	**362**

LUNCH

Hearty Vegetable Soup*	1 cup	95
Egg and Shrimp Salad*	1 serving	175
Tangy Seafood Cocktail Sauce*	1 tablespoon	—
Melon Ring with Raspberries	1 serving	85
Skim Milk	1 cup	88
	TOTAL	**443**

DINNER

Roast Turkey	1 slice	100
Baked Potato	1	50
Butter or Margarine	½ pat	38
Asparagus	6 stalks	20
Lemon Gelatin*	1 serving	—
Coffee or Tea (black or with artificial sweetener)	1 cup	—
	TOTAL	**208**

Buy a handsome new bathroom scale. It's good for morale and proof that you're serious.

TOTAL CALORIES: 1002

BREAKFAST

	Serving	Calories
Grapefruit Juice	½ cup	50
Shirred Egg*	1	100
Toast	1 slice	75
Skim Milk	1 cup	88
Coffee or Tea (black or with artificial sweetener)	1 cup	—
	TOTAL	**313**

LUNCH

Hearty Vegetable Soup*	1 cup	95
Crabmeat Salad*	½ cup	100
Celery Stuffed with Cottage Cheese*	1 stalk	25
Melba Toast	1 slice	16
Butter or Margarine	½ pat	38
Skim Milk	1 cup	88
	TOTAL	**362**

DINNER

Golden Peachy Chicken*	1 serving	205
Mashed Potatoes	½ cup	85
Diced Carrots	½ cup	25
Cucumber and Onion Salad*	1 serving	12
Coffee or Tea (black or with artificial sweetener)	1 cup	—
	TOTAL	**327**

TOTAL CALORIES: 994

BREAKFAST

	Serving	Calories
Sliced Orange	1	50
Scrambled Egg*	1	76
Toast	1 slice	75
Butter or Margarine	½ pat	38
Coffee or Tea (black or with artificial sweetener)	1 cup	—
	TOTAL	239

LUNCH

	Serving	Calories
Madrilene*	1 cup	50
Chef's Salad*	1 serving	205
Melba Toast	1 slice	16
Butter or Margarine	½ pat	38
Skim Milk	1 cup	88
Coffee or Tea (black or with artificial sweetener)	1 cup	—
	TOTAL	397

DINNER

	Serving	Calories
Cucumber Cocktail*	1 serving	—
Stuffed Baked Fish Fillets*	1 serving	125
Baked Potato	1	50
Asparagus	6 stalks	20
Cottage Salad*	1 serving	75
Skim Milk	1 cup	88
Coffee or Tea (black or with artificial sweetener)	1 cup	—
	TOTAL	358

TOTAL CALORIES: 1023

BREAKFAST

	Serving	Calories
Pineapple Juice, canned	½ cup	54
Soft-Boiled Egg	1	70
Toast	1 slice	75
Butter or Margarine	½ pat	38
Coffee or Tea (black or with artificial sweetener)	1 cup	—
	TOTAL	**237**

LUNCH

Minted Buttermilk Soup*	1 cup	85
Fruit Platter with Cheese*	1 serving	190
Melba Toast	1 slice	16
Butter or Margarine	½ pat	38
	TOTAL	**329**

DINNER

Spiced Veal Cutlet*	1	230
Baked Potato	1	50
Oriental Cauliflower*	1 serving	80
Shredded Lettuce	1 cup	9
Tomato Juice Dressing*	1 tablespoon	—
Skim Milk	1 cup	88
Coffee or Tea (black or with artificial sweetener)	1 cup	—
Lemon Gelatin	1 mold	—
	TOTAL	**457**

TOTAL CALORIES: 1008

BREAKFAST

	Serving	Calories
Grapefruit	½	44
Shirred Egg*	1	100
Toast	1 slice	75
Butter or Margarine	½ pat	38
Skim Milk	1 cup	88
Coffee or Tea (black or with artificial sweetener)	1 cup	—
	TOTAL	345

LUNCH

	Serving	Calories
Hearty Vegetable Soup*	1 cup	95
Stuffed Tomato Salad*	1 serving	60
Cottage Cheese	¼ cup	60
Melba Toast	1 slice	16
Butter or Margarine	½ pat	38
Raspberries	½ cup	46
Coffee or Tea (black or with artificial sweetener)	1 cup	—
	TOTAL	315

DINNER

	Serving	Calories
Cucumber Cocktail*	1 serving	—
Broiled Ground Beef (lean round steak)	3-ounce patty	185
Boiled Parsley Potato	1	50
Cooked Spinach	½ cup	25
Lemon Gelatin*	1 serving	—
Skim Milk	1 cup	88
Coffee or Tea (black or with artificial sweetener)	1 cup	—
	TOTAL	348

TOTAL CALORIES: 1016

BREAKFAST

	Serving	Calories
Raspberries	½ cup	46
Broiled Fresh Bass Fillet	1 (3″ x 7″ x ½″) piece	50
Toast	1 slice	75
Butter or Margarine	½ pat	38
Skim Milk	1 cup	88
Coffee or Tea (black or with artificial sweetener)	1 cup	—
	TOTAL	**297**

LUNCH

Clam-Tomato Cocktail*	1 serving	12
Omelet with Fine Herbs*	1 serving	200
Broccoli	½ cup	37
Melba Toast	1 slice	16
Butter or Margarine	½ pat	38
Tossed Green Salad	1 cup	15
Delight Salad Dressing*	1 tablespoon	3
Skim Milk	1 cup	88
	TOTAL	**409**

DINNER

Ovenburgers*	1 serving	165
Baked Potato	1	50
Carrots and Mushrooms*	½ cup	35
Stuffed Tomato Salad*	1 serving	60
Coffee or Tea (black or with artificial sweetener)	1 cup	—
	TOTAL	**310**

TOTAL CALORIES: 1004

BREAKFAST

	Serving	Calories
Tomato Juice	½ cup	28
Soft-Boiled Egg	1	70
Bread (toasted or plain)	1 slice	75
Butter or Margarine	½ pat	38
Coffee or Tea (black or with artificial sweetener)	1 cup	—
	TOTAL	**211**

LUNCH

Clear Beef Broth	1 cup	32
Rib Lamb Chop (lean)	1	100
String Beans	½ cup	22
White Enriched Bread	1 slice	75
Skim Milk	1 cup	88
Orange	1	50
	TOTAL	**367**

DINNER

Roast Chicken	2 slices	180
Cooked Kale	1/3 cup	20
Baked Potato (eat jacket also)	1	50
Skim Milk	1 cup	88
Butter or Margarine	½ pat	38
Vegetable Salad		
Lettuce Leaves	2	6
Green Pepper	¼	5
Cucumber	½	17
Celery	½ cup	13
Delight Salad Dressing*	3 tablespoons	9
Coffee or Tea (black or with artificial sweetener)	1 cup	—
	TOTAL	**426**

TOTAL CALORIES: 1033

BREAKFAST

	Serving	Calories
Grapefruit Sections (canned)	½ cup	90
Scrambled Egg*	1	76
Toast	1 slice	75
Butter or Margarine	½ pat	38
Skim Milk	1 cup	88
Coffee or Tea (black or with artificial sweetener)	1 cup	—
	TOTAL	**367**

LUNCH

	Serving	Calories
Chicken Salad Sandwich		
Chicken	3 ounces	170
Chopped Celery	1 tablespoon	—
Dieter's Mayonnaise*	1 tablespoon	15
Lettuce	1 leaf	—
Butter or Margarine	½ pat	38
Bread	2 slices	150
Skim Milk	1 cup	88
	TOTAL	**461**

DINNER

	Serving	Calories
Baked Codfish with Grapefruit*	1 serving	140
Baked Potato	1	50
Lettuce with Lemon Juice	¼ head	15
Coffee or Tea (black or with artificial sweetener	1 cup	—
	TOTAL	**205**

TOTAL CALORIES: 1001

BREAKFAST

	Serving	Calories
Orange-Grapefruit Juice	4-ounce glass	55
Poached Egg (use a non-stick pan, no fat)	1	70
Toast	1 slice	75
Butter or Margarine	½ pat	38
Skim Milk	1 cup	88
Coffee or Tea (black or with artificial sweetener)	1 cup	—
	TOTAL	326

LUNCH

Crabmeat Salad*	½ cup	100
Tomato and Watercress	1 serving	35
Hot French Bread	2"-thick slice	120
Butter or Margarine	½ pat	38
Melon Balls with Mint	¾ cup	40
Coffee or Tea (black or with artificial sweetener)	1 cup	—
	TOTAL	333

DINNER

Minted Buttermilk Soup*	1 cup	85
Broiled Frankfurter	1	115
Dieter's Potato Salad*	2/3 cup	100
Spiced Beets*	1/3 cup	30
Asparagus and Pimiento Salad*	1 serving	12
Coffee or Tea (black or with artificial sweetener)	1 cup	—
	TOTAL	342

TOTAL CALORIES: 1009

BREAKFAST

	Serving	Calories
Orange Juice	¾ cup	85
Poached Egg (use a non-stick pan, no fat)	1	70
Toast	1 slice	75
Butter or Margarine	½ pat	38
Coffee or Tea (black or with artificial sweetener)	1 cup	—
	TOTAL	268

LUNCH

Tuna Ring*	1 serving	250
Endive and Pepper Salad*	1 serving	55
Skim Milk	1 cup	88
	TOTAL	393

DINNER

Broiled Veal Chop	1/3 pound	200
Hot Potato Salad*	1 serving	60
Lemon-Chive Asparagus Spears*	1 serving	70
Stewed Rhubarb (with artificial sweetener)	½ cup	18
Coffee or Tea (black or with artificial sweetener)	1 cup	—
	TOTAL	348

TOTAL CALORIES: 1000

BREAKFAST

	Serving	Calories
Honeydew Melon	¼	75
Pan-Broiled Ham	1 thin slice	155
Toast	1 slice	75
Butter or Margarine	½ pat	38
Skim Milk	1 cup	88
Coffee or Tea (black or with artificial sweetener)	1 cup	—
	TOTAL	**431**

LUNCH

	Serving	Calories
Tomato-Celery Soup*	1 cup	—
Puffed Spanish Omelet*	1 serving	163
Green Salad		
Sliced Cucumber	½	15
Watercress	10 sprigs	2
Romaine	3 leaves	5
Vinegar Dressing*		
Melba Toast	1 slice	16
Coffee or Tea (black or with artificial sweetener)	1 cup	—
	TOTAL	**201**

DINNER

	Serving	Calories
Broiled Rock-Lobster Tails*	1 serving	160
Baked Potato	1	50
Butter or Margarine	½ pat	38
Cooked Spinach	½ cup	25
Fresh Peach	1	51
Skim Milk	½ cup	44
Coffee or Tea (black or with artificial sweetener)	1 cup	—
	TOTAL	**368**

Cut iced melon, apple or other fruits on the list into small pieces. Serve in clear glass stemware. It will look and feel like twice as much.

TOTAL CALORIES: 1004

BREAKFAST

	Serving	Calories
Orange Juice	¾ cup	85
Canadian-Style Bacon	1 slice	55
Toast	1 slice	75
Butter or Margarine	½ pat	38
Skim Milk	1 cup	88
Coffee or Tea (black or with artificial sweetener)	1 cup	—
	TOTAL	341

LUNCH

	Serving	Calories
Omelet with Fine Herbs*	1 serving	200
French Style Green Beans	½ cup	15
Spinach and Radish Salad*	1 serving	50
Skim Milk	1 cup	88
	TOTAL	353

DINNER

	Serving	Calories
Skewered Lamb and Pineapple*	1 skewer	180
Hot Potato Salad*	1 serving	60
Lemon-Chive Asparagus Spears*	1 serving	70
Coffee or Tea (black or with artificial sweetener)	1 cup	—
	TOTAL	310

TOTAL CALORIES: 1008

BREAKFAST

	Serving	Calories
Fruit Cocktail (canned in syrup)	½ cup	78
Soft-Boiled Egg	1	70
Toast	1 slice	75
Butter or Margarine	½ pat	38
Skim Milk	1 cup	88
Coffee or Tea (black or with artificial sweetener)	1 cup	—
	TOTAL	**349**

LUNCH

Mushroom Soup, Country Style*	1 cup	50
Stuffed Baked Fish Fillets*	1 serving	125
Oven French Fries*	½ cup	100
Coleslaw*	½ cup	25
Coffee Whip*	1 serving	—
	TOTAL	**300**

DINNER

Clear Broth	1 cup	—
Sukiyaki*	2/3 cup	220
Steamed Rice	¾ cup	102
Cucumber and Onion Salad*	1 serving	12
Lemon Mist*	1 serving	25
Jasmine Tea (no cream or sugar)	1 cup	—
	TOTAL	**359**

TOTAL CALORIES: 996

BREAKFAST

	Serving	Calories
Grapefruit (with liquid artificial sweetener)	½	44
Shredded Wheat (crisped in oven)	1 biscuit	85
Sugar	1 teaspoon	16
Skim Milk	1 cup	88
Coffee or Tea (black or with artificial sweetener)	1 cup	—
	TOTAL	**233**

LUNCH

Tomato Juice with Lemon	1 cup	50
Omelet with Fine Herbs*	1 serving	200
Green Beans	½ cup	22
Raw Carrots (shredded)	½ cup	25
Tossed Green Salad	1 cup	15
French Dressing*	1 tablespoon	50
Skim Milk	1 cup	88
	TOTAL	**450**

DINNER

Pan-Broiled Beef Liver*	1 slice	100
Mashed Potato	½ cup	85
Butter or Margarine	½ pat	38
Cooked Turnip Greens	½ cup	30
Beet and Onion Salad*	1 serving	60
Coffee or Tea (black or with artificial sweetener)	1 cup	—
	TOTAL	**313**

TOTAL CALORIES: 994

BREAKFAST

	Serving	Calories
Tomato Juice	½ cup	28
Soft-Boiled Egg	1	70
Toast	1 slice	75
Butter or Margarine	½ pat	38
Skim Milk	1 cup	88
Coffee or Tea (black or with artificial sweetener)	1 cup	—
	TOTAL	299

LUNCH

Minted Buttermilk Soup*	1 cup	85
Tuna Fish Salad*	½ cup	140
Melba Toast	1 slice	16
Butter or Margarine	½ pat	38
Raspberries	½ cup	46
Coffee or Tea (black or with artificial sweetener)	1 cup	—
	TOTAL	325

DINNER

Frankfurter Kabobs*	1 kabob	260
Hot Potato Salad*	1	60
Celery Stuffed with Cottage Cheese*	1 stalk	25
Coleslaw*	1 serving	25
Coffee or Tea (black or with artificial sweetener)	1 cup	—
	TOTAL	370

*Blindfolded tasters are fooled more often than
not in trying to identify low-calorie foods.
Don't advertise the fact that you are using
low-calorie dressings or other preparations.*

TOTAL CALORIES: 1032

BREAKFAST

	Serving		Calories
Fresh Peach	1 medium		45
Toast	1 slice		75
Butter or Margarine	½ pat		38
Skim Milk	1 cup		88
Coffee or Tea (black or with artificial sweetener)	1 cup		—
		TOTAL	246

LUNCH

	Serving		Calories
Chicken Pot Pie*	1 serving		335
Tossed Green Salad	1 cup		15
Delight Salad Dressing*	1 tablespoon		3
Iced Tea (with lemon or artificial sweetener)	1 glass		—
		TOTAL	353

DINNER

	Serving		Calories
Tuna Ring*	1 serving		250
Baked Potato	1		50
Spinach	1 cup		45
Skim Milk	1 cup		88
Coffee or Tea (black or with artificial sweetener)	1 cup		—
		TOTAL	433

TOTAL CALORIES: 1005

BREAKFAST

	Serving	Calories
Blueberries	½ cup	68
Scrambled Egg*	1	76
Toast	1 slice	75
Butter or Margarine	½ pat	38
Skim Milk	1 cup	88
Coffee or Tea (black or with artificial sweetener)	1 cup	—
	TOTAL	345

LUNCH

Clam-Tomato Cocktail*	1 cup	12
Chef's Salad*	1 serving	205
Apricot Fluff*	1 serving	40
Custard Sauce*	1 tablespoon	15
Skim Milk	1 cup	88
	TOTAL	360

DINNER

Mushroom Meat Loaf*	1 center slice	160
Boiled Parsley Potato	1	50
Butter or Margarine	½ pat	38
Cooked Green Beans	½ cup	22
Small Whole Cooked Onions	½ cup	30
Coffee or Tea (black or with artificial sweetener)	1 cup	—
	TOTAL	300

TOTAL CALORIES: 1031

BREAKFAST

	Serving		Calories
Raspberries	½ cup		35
Cornflakes	1 cup		95
Sugar	1 teaspoon		15
Skim Milk	1 cup		88
Coffee or Tea (black or with artificial sweetener)	1 cup		—
		TOTAL	233

LUNCH

	Serving		Calories
Poached Egg Supreme*	1 serving		205
Tossed Green Salad	1 cup		15
French Dressing	1 tablespoon		60
Skim Milk	1 cup		88
		TOTAL	368

DINNER

	Serving		Calories
Chicken a l'Orange*	1 serving		340
Baked Potato	1		50
Parsley Carrots	2		40
Coffee or Tea (black or with artificial sweetener)	1 cup		—
		TOTAL	430

NOTE: To reduce the calories in this menu, substitute 1 tablespoon Delight Salad Dressing* for the 1 tablespoon French Dressing. This would reduce the calorie count to 974.

TOTAL CALORIES: 1001

BREAKFAST

	Serving	Calories
Fresh Strawberries	½ cup	41
Hot Cereal	¾ cup	100
Sugar	1 teaspoon	16
Skim Milk	1 cup	88
Coffee or Tea (black or with artificial sweetener)	1 cup	—
	TOTAL	245

LUNCH

Mushroom Soup, Country Style*	1 cup	50
Egg and Shrimp Salad*	1 serving	175
Frozen Plum Creme*	1 serving	145
Coffee or Tea (black or with artificial sweetener	1 cup	—
	TOTAL	370

DINNER

Tomato Juice	½ cup	28
Broiled Sirloin Steak*	¼ pound	235
Parsley Carrots and Potatoes*	1 serving	105
Tossed Green Salad	1 cup	15
Delight Salad Dressing*	1 tablespoon	3
Coffee or Tea (black or with artificial sweetener)	1 cup	—
	TOTAL	386

TOTAL CALORIES: 1018

BREAKFAST

	Serving	Calories
Grapefruit Juice	1 cup	90
Toast	1 slice	75
Jam	1 teaspoon	20
Skim Milk	1 cup	88
Coffee or Tea (black or with artificial sweetener)	1 cup	—
	TOTAL	273

LUNCH

	Serving	Calories
Stuffed Tomato Salad*	1 serving	60
Hard-Boiled Egg	1	70
Melba Toast	1 slice	16
Butter or Margarine	½ pat	38
Skim Milk	1 cup	88
	TOTAL	272

DINNER

	Serving	Calories
Broiled Sirloin Steak	¼ pound	235
Baked Potato	1	50
Butter or Margarine	½ pat	38
Asparagus	1 cup	35
Fruit Salad*	1 serving	60
Lemon Fruit Dressing*	1 tablespoon	55
Coffee or Tea (black or with artificial sweetener)	1 cup	—
	TOTAL	473

TOTAL CALORIES: 1002

BREAKFAST

	Serving	Calories
Tomato Juice	1 cup	50
Poached Egg (use a non-stick pan, no fat)	1	70
Toast	1 slice	75
Butter or Margarine	½ pat	38
Skim Milk	1 cup	88
Coffee or Tea (black or with artificial sweetener)	1 cup	—
	TOTAL	321

LUNCH

	Serving	Calories
Roast Beef Sandwich		
Roast Beef	3 ounces	175
Rye Bread	1 slice	55
Tossed Green Salad	1 cup	15
Delight Salad Dressing*	1 tablespoon	3
Skim Milk	1 cup	88
	TOTAL	336

DINNER

	Serving	Calories
Spiced Veal Cutlet*	1 serving	230
Baked Potato	1	50
Parsley Carrots	2	40
Celery Stuffed with Cottage Cheese*	1 stalk	25
Coffee or Tea (black or with artificial sweetener)	1 cup	—
	TOTAL	345

TOTAL CALORIES: 1015

BREAKFAST

	Serving	Calories
Applesauce	½ cup	50
Soft-Boiled Egg	1	70
Toast	1 slice	75
Butter or Margarine	½ pat	38
Skim Milk	1 cup	88
Coffee or Tea (black or with artificial sweetener)	1 cup	—
	TOTAL	**321**

LUNCH

	Serving	Calories
Flounder and Horseradish Sauce*	1 serving	125
Spinach	1 cup	45
Coleslaw*	2/3 cup	70
Coffee or Tea (black or with artificial sweetener)	1 cup	—
	TOTAL	**240**

DINNER

	Serving	Calories
Russian Borscht*	1 cup	—
Dieter's Beef Stroganoff*	½ cup	240
Mixed Green Salad	1 cup	15
Delight Salad Dressing*	3 tablespoons	9
Steamed Rice	¾ cup	102
Skim Milk	1 cup	88
Coffee or Tea (black or with artificial sweetener)	1 cup	—
	TOTAL	**454**

TOTAL CALORIES: 1037

BREAKFAST

	Serving	Calories
Raspberries	½ cup	35
Soft-Boiled Egg	1	70
Toast	1 slice	75
Margarine	½ pat	38
Skim Milk	1 cup	88
Coffee or Tea (black or with artificial sweetener)	1 cup	—
	TOTAL	306

LUNCH

	Serving	Calories
Lime-Cabbage Salad*	1 serving	80
Dieter's Mayonnaise*	1 tablespoon	15
Uncreamed Cottage Cheese	½ cup	110
Maple Royal*	1 serving	110
Iced Tea (with lemon or artificial sweetener)	1 glass	—
	TOTAL	315

DINNER

	Serving	Calories
Fillet of Sole Valenciennes*	1 serving	150
Baked Potato	1	50
Butter or Margarine	½ pat	38
Beets	2/3 cup	45
Spinach	1 cup	45
Skim Milk	1 cup	88
Coffee or Tea (black or with artificial sweetener)	1 cup	—
	TOTAL	416

TOTAL CALORIES: 1025

BREAKFAST

	Serving	Calories
Orange Juice	¾ cup	85
Soft-Boiled Egg	1	70
Toast	1 slice	75
Butter or Margarine	½ pat	38
Skim Milk	1 cup	88
Coffee or Tea (black or with artificial sweetener)	1 cup	—
	TOTAL	356

LUNCH

	Serving	Calories
Hamburger (lean ground round)	3 ounces	200
Bread	2 slices	150
Butter or Margarine	½ pat	38
Dieter's Mayonnaise*	1 tablespoon	15
Mustard	to taste	—
Sliced Tomato	1 medium	30
Iced Tea (with lemon or artificial sweetener)	1 glass	—
	TOTAL	433

DINNER

	Serving	Calories
Russian Borscht*	1 serving	—
Pan-Broiled Liver*	1 serving	138
Baked Potato	1	50
Spinach	½ cup	25
Cantaloupe	¼	23
Coffee or Tea (black or with artificial sweetener)	1 cup	—
	TOTAL	236

TOTAL CALORIES: 1000

BREAKFAST

	Serving	Calories
Orange Juice	¾ cup	85
Poached Egg (use a non-stick pan, no fat)	1	70
Toast	1 slice	75
Butter or Margarine	½ pat	38
Skim Milk	1 cup	88
Coffee or Tea (black or with artificial sweetener)	1 cup	—
	TOTAL	356

LUNCH

	Serving	Calories
Clam-Tomato Cocktail*	1 serving	12
Veal and Mushroom Aspic*	1 serving	75
Spring Garden Salad*	1 serving	60
French Dressing*	1 tablespoon	50
Melba Toast	1 slice	16
Butter or Margarine	½ pat	38
Skim Milk	1 cup	88
	TOTAL	339

DINNER

	Serving	Calories
Roast Turkey	1 (4" x 2½" x ¼") slice	100
Cranberry Jelly*	1 serving	25
Mashed Potato	½ cup	85
Lemon-Chive Asparagus Spears*	1 serving	70
Grape Gelatin*	1 serving	25
Coffee or Tea (black or with artificial sweetener)	1 cup	—
	TOTAL	305

Invest in a blender. It will be one of your best friends in preparing nutritious fruit or vegetable cocktails, soups, aspics and salad dressings. A blender can whip cottage cheese into a dressing for your baked potato or green salad.

TOTAL CALORIES: 996

BREAKFAST

	Serving	Calories
Honeydew Melon	¼	75
Scrambled Egg*	1	76
Toast	1 slice	75
Butter or Margarine	½ pat	38
Skim Milk	1 cup	88
Coffee or Tea (black or with artificial sweetener)	1 cup	—
	TOTAL	**352**

LUNCH

	Serving	Calories
Mushroom Meat Loaf*	1 center slice 3½ ounces	160
Southern Green Beans*	1 serving	65
Mashed Potato (made with skim milk)	½ cup	85
Spring Garden Salad*	1 serving	60
Delight Salad Dressing*	1 tablespoon	3
Coffee or Tea (black or with artificial sweetener)	1 cup	—
	TOTAL	**373**

DINNER

	Serving	Calories
Flounder and Horseradish Sauce*	1 serving	125
Baked Mashed Squash*	1 serving	80
Fruit Salad*	1 serving	60
Fruit Salad Dressing*	1 tablespoon	6
Coffee or Tea (black or with artificial sweetener)	1 cup	—
	TOTAL	**271**

TOTAL CALORIES: 1025

BREAKFAST

	Serving	Calories
Tomato Juice	1 cup	**50**
Soft-Boiled Egg	1	**70**
Toast	1 slice	**75**
Butter or Margarine	½ pat	**38**
Skim Milk	1 cup	**88**
Coffee or Tea (black or with artificial sweetener)	1 cup	**—**
	TOTAL	**321**

LUNCH

	Serving	Calories
Cream of Chicken Soup (made with skim milk)	1 cup	**130**
Fruit Platter with Cheese*	1 serving	**190**
Toasted Melba Rounds	4	**36**
Coffee or Tea (black or with artificial sweetener)	1 cup	**—**
	TOTAL	**356**

DINNER

	Serving	Calories
Cucumber Cocktail*	1 serving	**—**
Braised Beef Roll-Ups*	1 serving	**260**
Baked Potato	1	**50**
Asparagus	6 stalks	**20**
Tossed Green Salad	1 cup	**15**
Delight Salad Dressing*	1 tablespoon	**3**
Lemon Gelatin*	1 serving	**—**
Coffee or Tea (black or with artificial sweetener)	1 cup	**—**
	TOTAL	**348**

TOTAL CALORIES: 1001

BREAKFAST

	Serving	Calories
Orange Juice	½ cup	75
Poached Egg (use a non-stick pan, no fat)	1	70
Toast	1 slice	75
Butter or Margarine	½ pat	38
Skim Milk	1 cup	88
Coffee or Tea (black or with artificial sweetener)	1 cup	—
	TOTAL	**346**

LUNCH

	Serving	Calories
Tomato Soup (plain)	½ cup	46
Broiled Frankfurter	1	115
Sauerkraut	½ cup	20
Lemon-Chive Asparagus Spears*	1 serving	70
Fresh Plum	1	56
Coffee or Tea (black or with artificial sweetener)	1 cup	—
	TOTAL	**307**

DINNER

	Serving	Calories
Beef Patties Burgundy*	1 serving	180
Scalloped Potatoes*	1 serving	125
Cooked Carrots	½ cup	25
Tossed Green Salad	1 cup	15
Delight Salad Dressing	1 tablespoon	3
Coffee or Tea (black or with artificial sweetener)	1 cup	—
	TOTAL	**348**

TOTAL CALORIES: 1024

BREAKFAST

	Serving		Calories
Strawberries (fresh or canned without sugar)	1 cup		**40**
Scrambled Egg*	1		**76**
Toast	1 slice		**75**
Butter or Margarine	½ pat		**38**
Skim Milk	1 cup		**88**
Coffee or Tea (black or with artificial sweetener)	1 cup		**—**
		TOTAL	**317**

LUNCH

	Serving		Calories
Chef's Salad*	1 serving		**205**
Melba Toast	1 slice		**16**
Butter or Margarine	½ pat		**38**
Skim Milk	1 cup		**88**
		TOTAL	**347**

DINNER

	Serving		Calories
Tomato Juice	1 cup		**50**
Beef Patties Burgundy*	1 serving		**180**
Baked Potato	1		**50**
Broccoli with Mustard Dill Sauce*	1 cup		**80**
Coffee or Tea (black or with artificial sweetener)	1 cup		**—**
		TOTAL	**360**

TOTAL CALORIES: 1006

BREAKFAST

	Serving	Calories
Pineapple Juice (canned)	½ cup	54
Deviled Egg*	2 halves	75
Toast	1 slice	75
Butter or Margarine	½ pat	38
Skim Milk	1 cup	88
Coffee or Tea (black or with artificial sweetener)	1 cup	—
	TOTAL	330

LUNCH

Salad Soup*	1 cup	12
Skewer of Chicken Livers and Tomato*	1 skewer	150
Cooked Diced Carrots	½ cup	25
Tossed Green Salad	1 cup	15
Delight Salad Dressing*	1 tablespoon	3
Pineapple-Mint Sherbet*	1 serving	45
Skim Milk	1 cup	88
	TOTAL	338

DINNER

Broiled Halibut Steak	1 (3″ x 1¼″ x 1″)	100
Lemon-Caper Sauce*	1 tablespoon	—
Baked Potato	1	50
Butter or Margarine	½ pat	38
Cooked Spinach	½ cup	25
Lime-Melon Mold*	1 serving	25
Pound Cake	1 (2″ x 2″ x ¼″) piece	100
Coffee or Tea (black or with artificial sweetener)	1 cup	—
	TOTAL	338

TOTAL CALORIES: 1005

BREAKFAST

	Serving	Calories
Tangerine Juice	4 ounces	55
French Toast (use a non-stick pan, no fat)	1 slice	100
Powdered Sugar	1 tablespoon	30
Skim Milk	1 cup	88
Coffee or Tea (black or with		
artificial sweetener)	1 cup	—
	TOTAL	**273**

LUNCH

Egg Bouillon*	1 serving	75
Open Club Sandwich		
Dieter's Mayonnaise*	1 tablespoon	15
Mustard	dash	—
Lettuce Leaf	—	—
Chicken	2 ounces	100
Swiss Cheese	1 slice	105
Rye Bread	1 slice	55
Coffee Whip*	1 serving	—
	TOTAL	**350**

DINNER

Golden Brown Chicken*	½ pound	215
Corn on Cob	1 medium ear	70
Butter or Margarine	½ pat	38
Baked Potato	1	50
Shredded Lettuce	1 cup	9
Tomato Juice Dressing*	1 tablespoon	—
Coffee or Tea (black or with		
artificial sweetener)	1 cup	—
	TOTAL	**382**

TOTAL CALORIES: 1003

BREAKFAST

	Serving	Calories
Blueberries	1 cup	85
Soft-Boiled Egg	1	70
Toast	1 slice	75
Butter or Margarine	½ pat	38
Coffee or Tea (black or with artificial sweetener)	1 cup	—
	TOTAL	**268**

LUNCH

	Serving	Calories
Tomato Juice	1 cup	50
Roast Chicken	3 ounces	150
Mashed Potato (made with skim milk)	½ cup	85
Green Beans	½ cup	22
Tossed Green Salad	1 cup	15
Delight Salad Dressing*	1 tablespoon	3
Skim Milk	1 cup	88
	TOTAL	**413**

DINNER

	Serving	Calories
Clear Broth	1 cup	—
Sukiyaki*	2/3 cup	220
Steamed Rice	¾ cup	102
Jasmine Tea (no sugar or cream)	1 cup	—
	TOTAL	**322**

TOTAL CALORIES: 1004

BREAKFAST

	Serving	Calories
Apricots	3 raw	55
Soft-Boiled Egg	1	70
Toast	1 slice	75
Butter or Margarine	½ pat	38
Skim Milk	1 cup	88
Coffee or Tea (black or with artificial sweetener)	1 cup	—
	TOTAL	**326**

LUNCH

Salmon Loaf with Mushroom Sauce*	1 serving	340
Cooked Spinach	½ cup	25
Coleslaw*	½ cup	25
Iced Tea with Lemon (no sugar)	1 glass	—
	TOTAL	**390**

DINNER

Tomato-Celery Soup*	1 cup	—
Rib Roast Beef	1 (5" x 2½" x ¼") slice	100
Baked Potato	1	50
Butter or Margarine	½ pat	38
Cooked Diced Carrots	½ cup	25
Cottage Salad*	1 serving	75
Coffee or Tea (black or with artificial sweetener)	1 cup	—
	TOTAL	**288**

Visualize the appearance of the meal. Think in terms of interesting, colorful arrangements with fruits, vegetables and salad greens.

TOTAL CALORIES: 1018

BREAKFAST

	Serving	Calories
Cantaloupe	½	60
Canadian-Style Bacon	2 medium slices	110
Toast	1 slice	75
Butter or Margarine	½ pat	38
Skim Milk	1 cup	88
Coffee or Tea (black or with artificial sweetener)	1 cup	—
	TOTAL	371

LUNCH

	Serving	Calories
Tomato Juice	1 cup	50
Egg and Shrimp Salad*	1 serving	175
Tangy Seafood Cocktail Sauce*	1 tablespoon	—
Coleslaw*	½ cup	25
Skim Milk	1 cup	88
	TOTAL	338

DINNER

	Serving	Calories
Roast Veal	1 (2″ x 2¾″ x ⅛″) slice	100
Potato	1	50
Butter or Margarine	½ pat	38
Sliced Beets	½ cup	46
Grated Carrot Salad	½ cup	25
Spanish Cream*	1 serving	50
Coffee or Tea (black or with artificial sweetener)	1 cup	—
	TOTAL	309

104

TOTAL CALORIES: 998

BREAKFAST

	Serving		Calories
Orange Juice	¾ cup		85
Toast	1 slice		75
Scrambled Egg*	1		76
Butter or Margarine	½ pat		38
Skim Milk	1 cup		88
Coffee or Tea (black or with artificial sweetener	1 cup		—
		TOTAL	362

LUNCH

	Serving		Calories
Salad Soup*	1 cup		12
Skewer of Chicken Livers and Tomato*	1 skewer		150
Broccoli with Lemon Juice	½ cup		37
Baked Acorn Squash*	1 serving		75
Skim Milk	1 cup		88
Coffee or Tea (black or with artificial sweetener)	1 cup		—
		TOTAL	362

DINNER

	Serving		Calories
Broiled Lamb Chop	1		100
Baked Potato	1		50
Butter or Margarine	½ pat		38
Mixed Green Salad	1 cup		15
Vinegar Dressing*			—
Spinach	½ cup		25
Raspberries	½ cup		46
Coffee or Tea (black or with artificial sweetener)	1 cup		—
		TOTAL	274

TOTAL CALORIES: 1001

BREAKFAST

	Serving	Calories
Fresh Pineapple	1"-thick slice	50
Toast	1 slice	75
Scrambled Egg*	1	76
Butter or Margarine	½ pat	38
Skim Milk	1 cup	88
Coffee or Tea (black or with artificial sweetener)	1 cup	—
	TOTAL	**327**

LUNCH

	Serving	Calories
Hearty Vegetable Soup*	1 cup	95
Ry-Krisp	1 triple cracker	23
Butter or Margarine	½ pat	38
Chef's Salad*	1 serving	205
Iced Tea with Lemon	1 glass	—
	TOTAL	**361**

DINNER

	Serving	Calories
Tomato Juice	1 cup	50
Broiled Sweetbreads (calf)	½ pair	120
Boiled Cabbage	1 cup	25
Spiced Beets*	1/3 cup	30
Skim Milk	1 cup	88
Coffee or Tea (black or with artificial sweetener)	1 cup	—
	TOTAL	**313**

TOTAL CALORIES: 1014

BREAKFAST

	Serving	Calories
Banana	½ banana	45
Wheat Flakes	¾ cup	100
Sugar	1 teaspoon	16
Skim Milk	½ cup	44
Coffee or Tea (black or with artificial sweetener)	1 cup	—
	TOTAL	205

LUNCH

	Serving	Calories
Tomato Juice	1 cup	50
Poached Egg Supreme*	1	205
Broccoli with Mustard Dill Sauce*	1 serving	80
Tossed Green Salad	1 cup	15
Delight Salad Dressing*	1 tablespoon	3
Skim Milk	1 cup	88
	TOTAL	441

DINNER

	Serving	Calories
Cold Roast Beef (lean)	1 (5" x 2½" x ¼") slice	100
Dieter's Potato Salad*	2/3 cup	100
Sliced Tomato	1	33
Celery Stuffed with Cottage Cheese*	2 stalks	50
Melon Ring with Raspberries*	1 ring with berries	85
Coffee or Tea (black or with artificial sweetener)	1 cup	—
	TOTAL	368

TOTAL CALORIES: 1012

BREAKFAST

	Serving	Calories
Orange Juice	¾ cup	85
Puffed Wheat	1 cup	45
Sugar	1 teaspoon	16
Skim Milk	1 cup	88
Coffee or Tea (black or with artificial sweetener)	1 cup	—
	TOTAL	234

LUNCH

	Serving	Calories
Puffed Spanish Omelet*	1 serving	163
Mixed Green Salad	1 cup	15
Vinegar Dressing*		—
Toasted English Muffin	1	140
Butter or Margarine	½ pat	38
Coffee or Tea (black or with artificial sweetener)	1 cup	—
	TOTAL	356

DINNER

	Serving	Calories
Chicken Florentine*	1 serving	219
Baked Potato	1	50
Spiced Beets*	1 serving	30
Tomato and Watercress	1 serving	35
Peaches in Sherry*	1 serving	88
Coffee or Tea (black or with artificial sweetener)	1 cup	—
	TOTAL	422

108

TOTAL CALORIES: 1004

BREAKFAST

	Serving	Calories
Melon Fruit Cup*	1 serving	50
Poached Egg (use a non-stick pan, no fat)	1	70
Toast	1 slice	75
Butter or Margarine	½ pat	38
Skim Milk	1 cup	88
Coffee or Tea (black or with artificial sweetener)	1 cup	—
	TOTAL	321

LUNCH

Tomato-Celery Soup*	1 cup	—
Chef's Salad*	1 serving	205
Ry-Krisp (seasoned and toasted)	1 triple cracker	25
Butter or Margarine	½ pat	38
Skim Milk	1 cup	88
Coffee or Tea (black or with artificial sweetener)	1 cup	—
	TOTAL	356

DINNER

Broiled Lamb Chop	1	100
Baked Potato	1	50
Diet Sour Cream*	1 tablespoon	20
Green Beans	½ cup	22
Tossed Green Salad	1 cup	15
Tomato Juice Dressing*	1 tablespoon	—
Cafe au Lait*	1 serving	120
	TOTAL	327

Never shop when you're hungry.
Wait until after lunch.

TOTAL CALORIES: 1006

BREAKFAST

	Serving	Calories
Tomato Juice	½ cup	28
Soft-Boiled Egg	1	70
Toast	1 slice	75
Butter or Margarine	½ pat	38
Skim Milk	1 cup	88
Coffee or Tea (black or with artificial sweetener)	1 cup	—
	TOTAL	**299**

LUNCH

Tuna Fish Salad*	1 serving	140
Relish Plate		
Carrots	½ cup	25
Radishes	5	10
Celery	3 stalks	13
Sweet Pickle	1	15
Citrus Salad*	1 serving	90
Iced Tea with Lemon and Mint	1 glass	—
	TOTAL	**293**

DINNER

Lamb Curry*	1 serving	228
Steamed Rice	¾ cup	102
Green Beans	½ cup	22
Mixed Green Salad	1 cup	15
Delight Salad Dressing*	1 tablespoon	3
Skim Milk	½ cup	44
Coffee or Tea (black or with artificial sweetener)	1 cup	—
	TOTAL	**414**

TOTAL CALORIES: 1003

BREAKFAST

	Serving	Calories
Banana	½ banana	45
Wheat Flakes	¾ cup	100
Sugar	1 teaspoon	16
Toast	1 slice	75
Butter or Margarine	½ pat	38
Skim Milk	1 cup	88
Coffee or Tea (black or with artificial sweetener)	1 cup	—
	TOTAL	**362**

LUNCH

Egg Bouillon*	1 cup	75
Oven Croquettes*	2	165
Green Beans	½ cup	22
Raw Carrots (shredded)	½ cup	25
Skim Milk	1 cup	88
	TOTAL	**375**

DINNER

Tomato Juice	1 cup	50
Broiled Lamb Chop	1	100
Baked Potato	1	50
Butter or Margarine	½ pat	38
Mixed Green Salad	1 cup	i5
Delight Salad Dressing*	1 tablespoon	3
Celery	3 stalks	10
Coffee or Tea (black or with artificial sweetener)	1 cup	—
	TOTAL	**266**

TOTAL CALORIES: 974

BREAKFAST

	Serving	Calories
Banana	½	45
Wheat Flakes	¾ cup	100
Sugar	1 teaspoon	16
Skim Milk	1 cup	88
Coffee or Tea (black or with artificial sweetener)	1 cup	—
	TOTAL	249

LUNCH

Egg Bouillon*	1 cup	75
Liverwurst Sandwich		
Liverwurst	1-ounce slice	85
Mustard		—
Rye Bread	2 slices	110
Melon-Ball Fruit Cup*	1 serving	50
Skim Milk	1 cup	88
Coffee or Tea (black or with artificial sweetener)	1 cup	—
	TOTAL	408

DINNER

Mushroom Meat Loaf*	1 serving	160
Baked Potato	1	50
Butter or Margarine	½ pat	38
Cooked Cauliflower	½ cup	31
Sliced Tomato	1	17
Watercress	1 cup	15
Vinegar Dressing*		—
Celery	2 stalks	6
Coffee or Tea (black or with artificial sweetener)	1 cup	—
	TOTAL	317

TOTAL CALORIES: 1007

BREAKFAST

	Serving	Calories
Cantaloupe	½	45
Hot Wheatena	2/3 cup	100
Sugar	1 teaspoon	16
Skim Milk	1 cup	88
Coffee or Tea (black or with artificial sweetener)	1 cup	—
	TOTAL	249

LUNCH

Clam-Tomato Cocktail*	1 serving	12
Egg and Shrimp Salad*	1 serving	175
Tangy Seafood Cocktail Sauce*		—
Toasted Ry-Krisp	2 triple crackers	40
Butter or Margarine	½ pat	38
Skim Milk	1 cup	88
	TOTAL	353

DINNER

Roast Turkey	1 (4″ x 2½″ x ¼″) slice	100
Cranberry-Orange Relish*		—
Baked Potato	1	50
Butter or Margarine	½ pat	38
Glazed Onions*	1 serving	110
Green Beans	½ cup	22
Fruit Salad*	1 serving	60
No-Calorie Fruit Dressing*		—
Celery Stuffed with Cottage Cheese	1 stalk	25
Coffee or Tea (black or with artificial sweetener)	1 cup	—
	TOTAL	405

You must exercise continually for one hour to burn up 200 calories. To lose one pound, you must burn up 3,500 calories. So obviously, diet is the only practical way of taking off weight.

TOTAL CALORIES: 1001

BREAKFAST

	Serving	Calories
Fresh Pineapple	1 slice	50
Hot Cereal	¾ cup	100
Sugar	1 teaspoon	16
Skim Milk	1 cup	88
Coffee or Tea (black or with artificial sweetener)	1 cup	—
	TOTAL	254

LUNCH

Clam-Tomato Cocktail*	1 serving	12
Swiss Luncheon Custard*	1 serving	268
Stuffed Tomato Salad*	1 serving	60
Coffee or Tea (black or with artificial sweetener)	1 cup	—
	TOTAL	340

DINNER

Fillet of Sole Veronique*	1 serving	219
Parsley Potato	1	50
Carrots and Mushrooms*	1 serving	35
Butter or Margarine	½ pat	38
Coleslaw*	1 serving	25
Apricot Fluff*	1 serving	40
Coffee or Tea (black or with artificial sweetener)	1 cup	—
	TOTAL	407

116

TOTAL CALORIES: 999

BREAKFAST

	Serving	Calories
Tomato Juice	1 cup	50
Soft-Boiled Egg	1	70
Toast	1 slice	75
Butter or Margarine	½ pat	38
Skim Milk	1 cup	88
Coffee or Tea (black or with artificial sweetener)	1 cup	—
	TOTAL	321

LUNCH

Crabmeat Bouillabaisse*	1 serving	200
Melba Toast	2 slices	32
Skim Milk	1 cup	88
	TOTAL	320

DINNER

Baked Codfish with Grapefruit*	1 serving	140
Cooked Onions	½ cup	40
Asparagus	1 cup	35
Endive and Pepper Salad*	1 serving	55
Baked Potato	1 medium	50
Butter or Margarine	½ pat	38
Coffee or Tea (black or with artificial sweetener)	1 cup	—
	TOTAL	358

TOTAL CALORIES: 1006

BREAKFAST

	Serving	Calories
Pear (canned in syrup)	2 halves	75
Soft-Boiled Egg	1	70
Toast	1 slice	75
Butter or Margarine	½ pat	38
Skim Milk	1 cup	88
Coffee or Tea (black or with artificial sweetener)	1 cup	—
	TOTAL	**346**

LUNCH

	Serving	Calories
Clear Broth	1 cup	—
Stuffed Green Peppers*	2 half peppers	250
Sliced Tomato and Watercress	1 serving	35
Skim Milk	1 cup	88
	TOTAL	**373**

DINNER

	Serving	Calories
Tomato Juice	1 cup	50
Broiled Lamb Chop (lean loin or rib)	1	100
Baked Potato	1	50
Butter or Margarine	½ pat	38
Broccoli	½ cup	37
Shredded Lettuce	1 cup	9
Delight Salad Dressing*	1 tablespoon	3
Coffee or Tea (black or with artificial sweetener)	1 cup	—
	TOTAL	**287**

TOTAL CALORIES: 994

BREAKFAST

	Serving	Calories
Apple Juice	½ cup	60
French Toast (use a non-stick pan, no fat)	1 slice	100
Confectioners' Sugar	1 teaspoon	21
Skim Milk	1 cup	88
Coffee or Tea (black or with artificial sweetener)	1 cup	—
	TOTAL	269

LUNCH

Mushroom Soup, Country Style*	1 cup	50
Orange-Cheese Salad*	1 serving	125
Ry-Krisp (seasoned and toasted)	2 triple crackers	50
Butter or Margarine	½ pat	38
Strawberries	½ cup	41
Coffee or Tea (black or with artificial sweetener)	1 cup	—
	TOTAL	304

DINNER

Tangy Barbecue Chicken*	1 serving	235
Parsley Carrots and Potatoes*	1 serving	105
Tossed Green Salad	1 cup	15
Delight Salad Dressing*	1 tablespoon	3
Double Apricot Souffle*	1 serving	63
Coffee or Tea (black or with artificial sweetener)	1 cup	—
	TOTAL	421

TOTAL CALORIES: 1004

BREAKFAST

	Serving	Calories
Orange Juice	¾ cup	85
Poached Egg	1	70
Toast	1 slice	75
Butter or Margarine	½ pat	38
Skim Milk	1 cup	88
Coffee or Tea (black or with artificial sweetener)	1 cup	—
	TOTAL	356

LUNCH

	Serving	Calories
Shrimp Salad		
Shrimp	3 ounces	110
Celery	¼ cup	5
Dieter's Mayonnaise*	1 tablespoon	15
Lettuce	2 leaves	—
Sliced Tomato	1 medium	30
Cantaloupe	½ medium	40
Skim Milk	1 cup	88
	TOTAL	288

DINNER

	Serving	Calories
Golden Peachy Chicken*	1 serving	205
Baked Potato	1	50
Butter or Margarine	½ pat	38
Green Beans	½ cup	22
Watercress	1 cup	15
French Dressing	½ tablespoon	30
Coffee or Tea (black or with artificial sweetener)	1 cup	—
	TOTAL	360

120

TOTAL CALORIES: 991

BREAKFAST

	Serving	Calories
Banana	½ medium	45
Shredded Wheat	1 biscuit	85
Sugar	1 teaspoon	16
Skim Milk	1 cup	88
Coffee or Tea (black or with artificial sweetener)	1 cup	—
	TOTAL	**234**

LUNCH

Mushroom Soup, Country Style*	1 cup	50
Baked Chicken Livers*	3	125
Steamed Rice	¾ cup	102
Green Beans	½ cup	22
Cucumber and Onion Salad*	1 serving	12
Coffee or Tea (black or with artificial sweetener)	1 cup	—
	TOTAL	**311**

DINNER

Tomato Juice	½ cup	28
Broiled Rock-Lobster Tails*	1 serving	160
Oven French Fries*	1 serving	100
Spinach	½ cup	25
Mixed Green Salad	1 cup	15
Delight Salad Dressing*	1 tablespoon	3
Hard-Boiled Egg	1	70
Pineapple-Mint Sherbet*	1 serving	45
Coffee or Tea (black or with artificial sweetener)	1 cup	—
	TOTAL	**446**

TOTAL CALORIES: 1001

BREAKFAST

	Serving	Calories
Pink Grapefruit (with artificial sweetener)	½	**44**
Oatmeal	2/3 cup	**107**
Sugar	1 teaspoon	**16**
Skim Milk	1 cup	**88**
Coffee or Tea (black or with artificial sweetener)	1 cup	**—**
	TOTAL	**255**

LUNCH

Madrilene*	1 serving	**50**
Chicken Salad*	1 serving	**180**
Asparagus	6 stalks	**20**
Butter or Margarine	½ pat	**38**
Skim Milk	1 cup	**88**
Iced Tea with Lemon	1 glass	**—**
	TOTAL	**376**

DINNER

Broiled Rock-Lobster Tails*	1 serving	**160**
Oven French Fries*	1 serving	**100**
Deviled Eggs*	2 halves	**75**
Carrots and Mushrooms*	½ cup	**35**
Coffee Whip*	1 serving	**—**
Coffee or Tea (black or with artificial sweetener)	1 cup	**—**
	TOTAL	**370**

122

Recipes

for

Delightful

Dieting

SHIRRED EGG
(Makes 1 serving)
100 calories per serving

1 tablespoon milk

1 medium egg

Salt and pepper to taste

¼ teaspoon butter or margarine

Paprika

Preheat oven to 325 degrees.
Lightly butter a shallow individual baking dish. Pour the milk into the dish; break the egg into it. (Some prefer to pour the milk over the egg.) Season to taste with salt and pepper. Dot with butter. Bake, uncovered, until egg is set, from 15 to 20 minutes. Garnish with paprika.

SCRAMBLED EGG
(Makes 1 serving)
76 calories per serving

1 egg

1 tablespoon skim milk

Salt and pepper to taste

Beat egg with wire whisk or fork in top of double boiler. Add milk, salt, and pepper. Cook over boiling water, stirring constantly, for 4 to 6 minutes.

POACHED EGG SUPREME
(Makes 1 serving)
205 calories per serving

1 medium slice Canadian-style bacon, 3″ diameter x ⅛″

1 egg

½ English muffin

Grill slice of Canadian bacon; drain on absorbent paper. Poach egg and toast the ½ English muffin. Place the bacon on the toasted muffin half. Top with the poached egg. Season to taste. Serve hot.

OMELET WITH FINE HERBS
(Makes 1 serving)
200 calories per serving

1 teaspoon salad oil or butter

2 medium eggs

2 tablespoons water

½ teaspoon herbs (chives, parsley, chervil, tarragon)

Salt and pepper

Heat oil or butter in 8-inch skillet over low heat. Beat eggs with the water; add herbs and seasonings. Prepare as in French Omelet.

DEVILED EGGS
(Makes 4 servings)
75 calories for 2 halves

4 hard-cooked eggs

1 tablespoon tomato juice

1½ teaspoons vinegar

1 teaspoon onion, grated

½ teaspoon dry mustard

½ teaspoon salt

⅛ teaspoon pepper

⅛ teaspoon liquid no-calorie sweetener

Dash of chili powder

Cool eggs; remove shells; cut eggs in half lengthwise; remove yolks. Mash yolks in small bowl; blend in all seasonings. Pile yolk mixture into egg whites.

EGG BOUILLON
(Makes 1 serving)
75 calories per serving

1 cup soup stock or 1 bouillon cube dissolved in 1 cup boiling water

1 egg

Salt and pepper to taste

Parsley, chopped

Bring soup stock to boiling point. Beat egg; pour into boiling stock, stirring constantly with fork; season to taste.

GOLDEN BROWN CHICKEN — Diet Style
(Makes 5 servings)
215 calories per 1/2-pound serving

2½-pound chicken, disjointed

2 teaspoons salad oil

1 teaspoon salt

¼ teaspoon pepper

Accent as desired

2 tablespoons flour

Preheat oven at 400 degrees for 20 minutes.
Wash and dry chicken. Place pieces in shallow pan, skin side up. Brush each piece lightly with salad oil. Combine seasonings, Accent, and flour; sift evenly over chicken. Pour ½ cup hot water into pan (add more later if needed). Bake, uncovered, until brown. Reduce heat to 300 degrees and continue baking, uncovered, until tender. Total cooking time is about 1 hour. After the first 30 minutes, baste chicken; baste once or twice again during cooking.

PUFFED SPANISH OMELET
(Makes 4 servings)
163 calories per serving

½ cup onion, chopped

½ cup green pepper, chopped

½ cup celery, chopped

¾ cup water

4 eggs, separated

½ cup canned tomatoes, drained and chopped

½ cup nonfat dry milk solids

½ teaspoon dried basil leaves

1 teaspoon salt

Dash of pepper

1 tablespoon butter or margarine

Preheat oven to 325 degrees.
Combine onion, green pepper, celery, and water in a saucepan. Simmer 15 to 20 minutes over moderately low heat (about 225 degrees) until tender. Drain. Beat egg whites in a large bowl until stiff but not dry. In another large bowl beat egg yolks until thick and lemon-colored. Add tomatoes, dry milk solids, basil, salt, and pepper to egg yolks; beat until blended. Fold in cooked vegetables and beaten egg whites. In a heavy 8-inch skillet with an ovenproof handle melt butter over moderately high heat (about 275 degrees) until butter starts to foam. Add egg mixture and cook 10 minutes or until omelet puffs up and is lightly browned on the bottom. Place omelet in oven and bake 15 to 17 minutes, until top is dry and lightly browned. Cut into wedges to serve.

126

Figure out the caloric and carbohydrate worth of what you're eating, and if you're over your allotment for a day, cut down the following day. Make sure that at the end of the week you're on schedule.

CHERRY FRUIT SALAD
(Makes 4 servings)
30 calories per serving

1 envelope low-calorie cherry-flavored gelatin

⅛ teaspoon salt

⅛ teaspoon ground cloves

⅛ teaspoon cinnamon

2 cups boiling water

¼ cup unsweetened cherries, pitted and quartered

2/3 medium banana, sliced

Combine gelatin, salt, cloves, and cinnamon. Add boiling water; stir to dissolve. Chill until thickened. Fold in fruit. Pour into 4 individual molds. Chill until firm. Unmold on serving plates.

EGG AND SHRIMP SALAD
(Makes 1 serving)
175 calories per serving

Arrange 6 cleaned, cooked or canned shrimp on bed of lettuce; garnish with 1 hard-cooked egg, quartered. Serve with Tangy Seafood Cocktail Sauce.*

ENDIVE AND PEPPER SALAD
(Makes 8 servings)
55 calories per serving

3 tablespoons vegetable oil

1 green pepper, sliced

6 scallions, finely chopped

2 tablespoons vinegar

2 tablespoons water

¾ teaspoon salt

1 bunch curly endive, cut into pieces

Heat vegetable oil in skillet. Add green pepper and scallions. Saute until tender. Remove from heat. Stir in vinegar, water, and salt. Return to heat and bring to a boil. Pour over endive and toss gently.

TOMATO ASPIC SALAD
(Makes 4 servings)
30 calories per individual mold

1 envelope unflavored gelatin

¼ cup cold water

1½ cups hot tomato juice

1 tablespoon onion, grated

1 tablespoon lemon juice

¼ teaspoon Worcestershire sauce

Dash of pepper

Salad greens

Soften gelatin in cold water; dissolve in hot tomato juice. Add seasonings and blend. Pour into 4 individual molds. Chill until firm. Unmold on salad greens. No salad dressing is required.

SPRING GARDEN SALAD
(Makes 12 servings)
60 calories per serving

12 small firm tomatoes

1 package (3 ounces) lemon gelatin

1 cup boiling water

¾ cup cold water

¼ cup lemon juice

½ teaspoon celery salt

1½ cups cucumber, finely chopped

1 tablespoon onion, chopped

Lettuce

Slice stem end and scoop out center of tomatoes. Set aside. Dissolve lemon gelatin in boiling water. Stir in cold water, lemon juice, and celery salt. Chill until slightly thickened. Fold in cucumber and onion. Spoon gelatin mixture into tomatoes. Chill until set. Serve on lettuce.

FRUIT SALAD
(Makes 8 servings)
60 calories per serving

2 cups apple, diced

2 cups grapefruit sections

1 cup banana, sliced

1 cup peach, sliced

Lettuce

Combine ingredients, toss, and serve on lettuce.

√TUNA FISH SALAD
(Makes 4 servings)
140 calories per 1/2-cup serving

1 cup canned tuna fish, drained

1 egg, hard-cooked and chopped

½ cup celery, diced

¼ cup cucumber, diced

1 2-inch-long sweet pickle, chopped

Salt to taste

Dash of pepper

1½ teaspoons lemon juice

2 tablespoons Dieter's Mayonnaise*

¼ head lettuce

Drain tuna fish. Flake fish into medium bowl. Add egg, celery, cucumber, pickle, and seasonings. Sprinkle with lemon juice; mix in the mayonnaise, and chill. To serve, mound on crisp lettuce.

NOTE: If all oil is washed off tuna fish, the calorie count will be lower. If dietetic-pack tuna, which is canned without oil, is used, the calorie count of a ½-cup serving of salad will be about 85.

SALMON SALAD: Canned salmon may be used in place of tuna. Individual serving of ½ cup will be 135 calories.

Be creative with garnishes such as parsley, watercress, lemon slices or a rosebud radish. Paprika also perks up dull-looking foods.

LIME-CABBAGE SALAD
(Makes 6 servings)
80 calories per serving

1 package (3 ounces) lime gelatin

1 cup boiling water

½ cup cold water

3 tablespoons lemon juice

¾ cup cabbage, shredded

½ cup crushed pineapple, undrained

1 tablespoon pimiento, chopped

Lettuce

Dissolve Lime Gelatin in boiling water. Add cold water and lemon juice. Chill until mixture is slightly thickened. Add cabbage, crushed pineapple, and chopped pimiento. Pour into individual molds or a square pan. Chill until firm. Unmold. Serve on lettuce.

STUFFED TOMATO SALAD
(Makes 1 serving)
60 calories per serving

Stuffing:

¼ cup celery, diced

¼ cup cabbage, shredded

2 small radishes, sliced

1 small tomato, peeled and quartered but not cut through

Lettuce

Parsley sprigs

1 tablespoon Dieter's Mayonnaise*

Mix the vegetables for stuffing with the mayonnaise. Arrange tomato on lettuce leaves; push the quarters apart and fill with the stuffing. Garnish with parsley sprigs.

CHICKEN SALAD
(Makes 1 serving)
180 calories per serving

½ cup chicken, cooked

¼ cup celery, diced

¼ cucumber, diced

Salt, pepper, paprika, celery seed, onion juice to taste

1 tablespoon Dieter's Mayonnaise*

Lettuce

Dice chicken. Add diced vegetables and season to taste; add mayonnaise. Serve on crisp lettuce. Turkey may be substituted for chicken.

✓ COTTAGE SALAD
(Makes 9 servings)
75 calories per serving

1 package (3 ounces) lemon gelatin

1 teaspoon salt

1¼ cups boiling water

2 tablespoons vinegar

2 teaspoons onion, grated

1½ cups uncreamed cottage cheese

½ cup green pepper, chopped

Lettuce

Combine gelatin and salt; dissolve in boiling water. Stir in vinegar and onion. Chill until slightly thickened. Beat in cottage cheese until well blended; fold in green pepper. Pour into a 9-inch pan. Chill until firm. Cut into squares to serve on lettuce. Garnish with pimiento cut-outs or green pepper rings.

TOMATO CATSUP SALAD DRESSING
(Makes about 2 cups; 1 tablespoon equals 1 serving)
75 calories per serving

1 cup vegetable oil

1/3 cup cider vinegar

½ cup catsup

¼ cup sugar

2 teaspoons dry mustard

1 teaspoon salt

1 teaspoon Worcestershire sauce

½ teaspoon pepper

Salad greens

Measure ingredients into blender; cover and blend at high speed about 1 minute. Serve over salad greens.

BEET AND ONION SALAD
(Makes 1 serving)
60 calories per serving

1/3 cup beets, cooked or canned, drained and sliced

Chicory

1 onion or scallion, sliced

½ tablespoon French dressing

Arrange sliced beets on bed of chicory; top with the sliced onion, including part of the top. Drizzle the French dressing over all.

✓DIETER'S POTATO SALAD
(Makes 6 servings)
100 calories per 2/3-cup serving

3 cups potatoes, cooked and diced	1 to 1½ teaspoons salt
2 medium hard-cooked eggs, diced	Dash of pepper or paprika
½ cucumber, diced	1/3 cup Dieter's Mayonnaise*
½ cup celery, diced	1 head Boston lettuce
½ small onion, chopped	

Mix and chill all ingredients except lettuce. To serve, arrange portions in lettuce cups; or serve on a lettuce-bordered platter.

SPINACH AND RADISH SALAD
(Makes 8 servings)
50 calories per serving

6 cups fresh spinach

1½ cups radishes, sliced

1 cup onions, sliced

¼ cup Tomato Catsup Salad Dressing*

Combine spinach, radishes, and onions until well mixed. Toss with Tomato Catsup Dressing.*

CRABMEAT SALAD
(Makes 3 servings)
100 calories per 1/2-cup serving

7½ ounce can crabmeat

½ cup celery, finely minced

2 tablespoons green pepper, chopped

4 small radishes, sliced

1 tablespoon lemon juice

Salt to taste

Dash of pepper

¼ cup Dieter's Mayonnaise*

Chicory

Drain and flake crabmeat. Combine with the prepared vegetables; add lemon juice. Season to taste with salt and pepper. Chill. Just before serving, mix in the mayonnaise. Serve on chicory.

ORANGE-CHEESE SALAD
(Makes 4 servings)
125 calories per serving

2 cups cottage cheese

1 tablespoon fresh mint, chopped

¼ teaspoon nutmeg

2 oranges, peeled and thinly sliced

Curly endive, watercress, or lettuce

No-Calorie Fruit Dressing*

Mix together cottage cheese, mint, and nutmeg; form into small balls. Arrange ¼ of the balls of cheese and slices from ½ orange on salad greens of choice. Serve with No-Calorie Fruit Dressing.*

√CITRUS SALAD
(Makes 6 servings)
90 calories per serving

1 package (3 ounces) lime gelatin

1 cup boiling water

1 cup cold water

1¼ cups (1-pound can) grapefruit and orange sections, drained

Dissolve lime gelatin in boiling water. Stir in cold water. Chill until slightly thickened. Fold in grapefruit and orange sections. Pour into 3-cup mold. Chill until firm.

CHEF'S SALAD
(Makes 1 serving)
205 calories per serving

Salad greens as desired

1 celery heart, diced

1 tablespoon French dressing

1 small tomato, quartered

1 ounce chicken, cut into strips

½ ounce process American cheese, cut into strips

Break chilled salad greens into salad bowl. Add celery. Pour dressing over greens and celery and toss lightly. Arrange quartered tomato, chicken and cheese strips over top of greens. Serve.

✓ COLESLAW
(Makes 1/2 cup serving)
25 calories per serving

½ teaspoon onion, minced (optional)

1 tablespoon Dieter's Mayonnaise*

½ cup cabbage, shredded

Parsley

Add minced onion to the mayonnaise, if desired. Toss cabbage with the mayonnaise. Garnish with parsley. (The parsley may be chopped and added to the cabbage.)

For variation, use half green cabbage and half red cabbage for the slaw. Add 2 tablespoons chopped green pepper or chopped cucumber to the cabbage.

ASPARAGUS AND PIMIENTO SALAD
(Makes 4 servings)
12 calories per serving

1 pound (about 16 spears) cooked asparagus, drained and chilled; or

    1 can (1 pound, 4 ounces) green asparagus tips

Vinegar Dressing*

Pimiento strips

Marinate asparagus 1 hour in Vinegar Dressing.* Arrange in 4 bundles, circled by strips of pimiento; serve each in lettuce cup or on watercress with 1 tablespoon Vinegar Dressing* mixed with ¼ teaspoon capers.

CHUNKY GAZPACHO
(Makes 4 servings)
50 calories per serving

2 large tomatoes, peeled and coarsely chopped

1 small cucumber, peeled and coarsely chopped

½ medium onion, finely chopped

1 small green pepper, chopped

1 cup tomato juice

1 tablespoon vinegar

½ teaspoon salt

⅛ teaspoon pepper

In large bowl, stir all ingredients until well combined. Cover and refrigerate 2 hours or until icy cold. Serve in soup bowls.

CELERY STUFFED WITH COTTAGE CHEESE
(Makes 2 servings)
25 calories per individual serving of 1 stalk

2 medium stalks celery

1 teaspoon parsley, chopped

2 tablespoons cottage cheese

Paprika

Celery stalks should be crisp and dry. If small inner stalks are used, do not remove leaves. Mix chopped parsley with cottage cheese; stuff the celery with the cheese; chill well. Before serving, sprinkle cheese with paprika.

✓ FILLET OF SOLE VALENCIENNES
(Makes 6 servings)
150 calories per serving

¼ cup onion, chopped

2 cups fresh mushrooms, sliced

2 tablespoons margarine

2 pounds fillet of flounder

2 tablespoons lemon juice

1 tablespoon parsley, chopped

1 teaspoon oregano

⅛ teaspoon pepper

Saute onion and mushrooms in margarine until tender in a large skillet. Layer flounder in pan and sprinkle remaining ingredients over fish. Cover and simmer gently 20 minutes.

136

MIXED VEGETABLE SALAD
(Makes 4 servings)
15 calories per serving

Marinate together for about 1 hour equal amounts of cooked and diced carrots, string beans cut into 1½-inch strips, asparagus tips, and a small amount of minced onion in Vinegar Dressing,* Spiced Vinegar,* or Barbecue Dressing.* Serve on lettuce leaves or watercress.

CUCUMBER AND ONION SALAD
(Makes 3 servings)
12 calories per serving

¼ cup vinegar

2 tablespoons water

¼ teaspoon salt

¼ teaspoon liquid no-calorie sweetener

1 teaspoon mint or parsley, chopped (if desired)

Paprika

Pepper

1 cucumber, thinly sliced

1 onion, thinly sliced

Combine vinegar, water, salt, sweetener, paprika, and pepper in medium-sized bowl; add cucumber and onion. Chill in refrigerator to blend flavors. Serve cold; garnish with mint or parsley.

FRUIT PLATTER WITH CHEESE
(Makes 2 servings)
190 calories per serving

1 medium fresh peach, peeled and quartered

½ medium banana, cut into chunks

¼ cup sweet, fresh cherries, pitted

1 cup (about 12) honeydew melon balls

1 cup watercress

2 slices process American cheese, cut into triangles

Arrange fruit in an attractive pattern on a platter. Tuck in the watercress sprigs. Arrange cheese triangles at edge of platter. Cottage cheese (1 cup) may be used in place of the American cheese.

SPICED VEAL CUTLET
(Makes 4 servings)
230 calories per 3-ounce serving

1 pound veal cutlet

1 clove garlic

1 tablespoon flour

1 teaspoon seasoned salt

Pinch of herbs (sage, thyme, basil), crushed

1 tablespoon salad oil

½ cup water

1 teaspoon Worcestershire sauce

Lemon slices

Rub surface of meat with cut garlic clove. Mix flour, seasoned salt, and just a pinch of desired herbs. Sprinkle both sides of meat with the mixture. Heat salad oil in skillet; brown meat slowly on both sides; watch carefully that it does not burn. Add hot water and Worcestershire sauce. Simmer, covered, until tender, about 45 minutes. Serve with lemon slices.

FLOUNDER AND HORSERADISH SAUCE
(Makes 4 servings)
125 calories per serving

2 cups water	2 teaspoons salt
4 onion slices	1½ pounds fillet of flounder
1 carrot	1 tablespoon margarine
2 sprigs parsley	4 teaspoons flour
1 bay leaf	1½ to 2 tablespoons horseradish, drained

Combine water, onion, carrot, parsley, bay leaf, and salt; simmer 10 minutes. Roll fillets and drop into stock. Simmer 10 to 12 minutes or until fish turns white and flakes easily. Remove from liquid; reserve 1 cup stock. Add additional water if necessary.

Melt margarine; stir in flour until well blended. Gradually add reserved fish stock, stirring constantly. Simmer 10 minutes or until liquid is of sauce consistency. Remove from heat and stir in horseradish. Serve with fish.

To make a more satisfying food of skim milk, boil and then cool before using. Boiled skim milk is much more filling.

OVENBURGERS
(Makes 6 servings)
165 calories per ovenburger

2 tablespoons onion, chopped

1¼ pounds lean ground round steak

½ cup soft bread crumbs (made from 1 slice bread)

2 tablespoons catsup

1 teaspoon salt

⅛ teaspoon pepper

½ teaspoon Worcestershire sauce

1 medium egg

Preheat oven to 350 degrees.

Combine onion, ground beef, bread crumbs, and seasonings. Add egg and blend well. Form meat mixture into 6 round cakes and place in a shallow baking dish. Bake about 25 minutes.

For variation, horseradish or prepared mustard may be used in place of onions. Or combine the meat with only bread crumbs and egg and serve with a barbecue sauce.

STUFFED BAKED FISH FILLETS
(Makes 4 servings)
125 calories per serving

1 tablespoon butter or margarine

1 clove garlic, minced

4 fish fillets (about 1 pound)

Salt and pepper to taste

Mushroom Stuffing (recipe below)

1 cup tomato sauce

Lemon wedges

Preheat oven to 350 degrees.

Melt butter or margarine; stir in garlic. Dry fillets; brush with garlic butter; sprinkle with salt and pepper. Fill each fillet with 1 tablespoon Mushroom Stuffing; roll; fasten with wooden picks. Place 1 inch apart in shallow baking pan; pour over tomato sauce. Bake about 30 minutes. Serve hot with wedge of lemon.

MUSHROOM STUFFING
(Makes 1/2 cup)
100 calories per 1/2 cup

¾ cup mushrooms, chopped

1 tablespoon onion, grated

1 tablespoon butter or margarine

2 tablespoons parsley, minced

½ teaspoon poultry seasoning

¼ teaspoon salt

Dash of cayenne

Saute mushrooms and onion in butter or margarine 5 minutes or until onion is tender and yellow. Mix in parsley, poultry seasoning, salt, and cayenne. Use as stuffing for fish or meat.

BAKED CHICKEN LIVERS
(Makes 3 servings)
125 calories per serving of 3 chicken livers

9 chicken livers

Sprinkle of seasoning

1 teaspoon flour

1 teaspoon butter

Preheat oven 10 minutes at 400 degrees.

Wash chicken livers; season. Sift over light sprinkling of flour; dot with butter. Place in a shallow pan. Bake 25 minutes.

SKEWER OF CHICKEN LIVERS AND TOMATO
(Makes 1 serving)
150 calories per serving

3 3-ounce chicken livers

Salt

½ teaspoon flour

1 small tomato

¼ teaspoon butter or margarine

Preheat oven 10 minutes at 400 degrees.

Wash chicken livers, salt lightly, sift over thin sprinkling of flour. Wash tomato and quarter. Arrange on skewer, alternating chicken livers with tomato quarters. Dot with butter. Place skewer in shallow pan. Bake 20 minutes.

FRANKFURTER KABOBS
(Makes 4 servings)
260 calories per serving

4 5½-inch-long frankfurters, quartered

4 medium onions, sliced

2 medium tomatoes, quartered

8 whole raw mushrooms

Barbecue sauce:

    1½ teaspoon butter or margarine

    ¼ cup green pepper, chopped

    1 small onion, chopped

    ½ cup chili sauce

    1 drop of tabasco

    ½ teaspoon salt

    Dash of pepper

Preheat oven 10 minutes at 350 degrees.

To make barbecue sauce, melt butter in a small skillet; cook the green pepper and onion about 3 minutes; add chili sauce and seasonings. Simmer about 8 minutes. Put frankfurters in hot water for a minute or two; drain and dry. Prepare kabobs by arranging alternately on 4 skewers pieces of the quartered frankfurters, onion slices, tomato wedges, and mushrooms. Broil under medium heat, turning to lightly brown all sides. Spread with half the sauce; broil 5 minutes. Turn; spread with the rest of the sauce, and broil 5 minutes longer. To catch the drippings place a pan beneath the skewers or line the broiler pan with foil.

√ GOLDEN PEACHY CHICKEN
(Makes 8 servings)
205 calories per serving

2 2½-pound fryers, cut up

¼ cup peach syrup

2 tablespoons lemon juice

1 teaspoon soy sauce

2 tablespoons margarine

8 peach halves

Preheat oven to 375 degrees.

Arrange chicken pieces in single layer in a shallow roasting pan.Combine peach syrup, lemon juice, and soy sauce. Pour over chicken. Dot with margarine. Bake until chicken is done, about 1½ hours, basting frequently. Thirty minutes before chicken is done, place peach halves around chicken. Serve chicken garnished with peaches.

Cook foods in as little water as possible and just barely long enough to make them tender. They satisfy hunger best that way and you also save more vitamins and other protective elements.

PAN-BROILED LIVER
(Makes 1 serving)
138 calories per serving

1 slice beef liver, 3½" x 2½" x ⅜"   Salt and pepper to taste

½ pat butter or margarine

Place liver in heated pan and cover with boiling water. Cover pan and let stand 12 minutes. Remove liver and drain off water. Melt butter or margarine in pan. Add liver and cook about 1 minute on each side.

CRABMEAT AND ORANGE CREPES
(Makes 6 servings)
234 calories per serving

2 eggs

1 can (10½ ounces) low-calorie mandarin oranges

Skim milk

1 cup all-purpose flour

Dash of salt

2 tablespoons butter, melted

1 can (10½ ounces) condensed chicken broth

1 tablespoon cornstarch

2 tablespoons low-calorie tomato catsup

2 cups fresh, frozen, or canned crabmeat, drained and flaked

1 can (5 ounces) water chestnuts, drained and diced

Preheat oven to 400 degrees

Beat eggs until yolks and whites are blended. Drain oranges and save juice. Add enough milk to juice to make 1 cup. Beat mixture into eggs. Add flour and salt, and beat until smooth as heavy cream. Brush a 6-inch skillet lightly with a little of the melted butter. Spoon in about two tablespoons of batter and rotate pan to coat bottom evenly. Brown lightly; turn crepe with spatula and brown on other side. Repeat, making 18 crepes. Stack cooked crepes until ready to use. Now, in a saucepan, stir chicken broth into cornstarch. Add catsup. Cook over low heat, stirring constantly until sauce bubbles and thickens. Fold in crabmeat, water chestnuts, and oranges. Fill crepes with crab mixture. Roll up crepes and place side by side in a single layer in a greased, shallow casserole. Bake 15 to 20 minutes or until hot.

BROILED ROCK-LOBSTER TAILS
(Makes 4 servings)
160 calories per serving

4 rock-lobster tails (about 8 ounces each)

1 tablespoon butter or margarine, melted

¼ teaspoon onion salt

Salt and pepper to taste

Preheat broiler.

Cut around under-shell membrane of rock-lobster tail with kitchen scissors; remove membrane; bend back tail until back shell cracks to prevent curling during broiling. Place on broiler rack, shell side up; broil with top of shellfish 3 inches from unit or tip of flame 6 minutes. Turn; brush flesh side with melted butter or margarine mixed with onion salt, sprinkle with salt and pepper and broil about 8 minutes or until lobster is cooked through. Serve hot with Lemon-Caper Sauce.*

SWEET AND SOUR SHRIMP
(Makes 6 servings)
200 calories per serving

1 can (15½ ounces) low-calorie pineapple chunks

2 tablespoons peanut oil

4 scallions, trimmed and chopped

1 cup celery, sliced

¼ cup pimiento, diced

2 tablespoons cornstarch

1 cup chicken broth

1 tablespoon soy sauce

1 tablespoon sugar

2 tablespoons vinegar

1 can (1 pound) bean sprouts, drained

2 pounds medium-sized cooked shrimp, shelled and deveined

Drain pineapple; reserve juice and add enough water to it to make 1 cup. Heat oil and saute scallions, celery, and pimiento until limp. Sprinkle with cornstarch. Stir in pineapple juice and chicken broth. Cook, stirring all the while, until sauce thickens. Stir in soy sauce, sugar, and vinegar. Add bean sprouts, shrimp, and pineapple.

BROILED SIRLOIN STEAK
235 calories per serving

Choose a steak at least ¾ of an inch thick. Bring to room temperature before broiling. Turn regulator of stove to "broil" and fully preheat broiler. Trim excess fat from the steak and slash fat edges in several places to prevent curling. Place steak on rack; place under heat unit so that top of meat is from 3 to 3½ inches under heat. Follow directions of stove manufacturer as to whether door to broiling unit should be left partially open during the broiling process.

Broil top side for half the required time; season the cooked side. Turn steak once, using a wide or spreading spatula, never a fork. Broil the other side for the rest of the required time. Individual serving is ¼-pound piece, 4" x 2" x 1", lean meat only.

Time Required to Broil Steak

Thickness	Rare	Medium
¾" to 1"	8 to 10 minutes	12 to 14 minutes
1½"	14 to 16 minutes	18 to 20 minutes
2"	35 to 40 minutes	45 to 50 minutes

CHINESE-STYLE BEEF AND VEGETABLES
(Makes 4 servings)
330 calories per serving

1 tablespoon cornstarch

2 tablespoons soy sauce

1 pound round steak, cut into ¼-inch-thick strips

2 tablespoons salad oil

1 package (7 ounces) snow peas, thawed

2 tablespoons vinegar

1 tablespoon sugar

10 to 12 radishes, thinly sliced

Prepare about 30 minutes before serving.

In medium bowl, mix cornstarch and soy sauce; add meat and toss until well coated. In medium skillet over medium-high heat, cook meat in hot oil, stirring constantly, until lightly browned. Cover and cook over low heat 10 minutes or until tender. Add snow peas, vinegar, and sugar; cook, stirring constantly, 2 minutes or until snow peas are tender-crisp. Add radishes and heat through. Serve immediately (radishes will lose color if left standing).

MUSHROOM MEAT LOAF
(Makes a 2-pound loaf)
160 calories per 3-1/2-ounce serving

½ cup fresh mushrooms, sliced

2 tablespoons onion, minced

2 tablespoons green pepper, chopped

½ cup celery, chopped

1 egg, beaten

¼ cup milk

½ cup soft bread crumbs (made from 1 slice bread)

1 tablespoon catsup

1 tablespoon Worcestershire sauce

2 teaspoons salt

Pepper

2 pounds lean ground chuck

Preheat oven to 400 degrees.

Chop vegetables with the bread. In a small bowl beat egg; add milk, catsup, Worcestershire sauce, and seasonings. Combine mixtures with ground chuck and blend well. Form into a loaf; place on rack in baking pan with cover. Pour ½ cup hot water into pan; cover and bake 1 hour. Remove cover the last 15 minutes of baking to brown top of loaf. (If desired, loaf may be baked in an oven-glass bread pan. Omit the water. Cover loaf with aluminum foil the first 45 minutes.) On removing from oven, drain off all drippings. Serve hot or cold.

VEAL AND MUSHROOM ASPIC
(Makes 6 servings)
75 calories per serving

1 envelope unflavored gelatin

1 can (12 ounces) mixed vegetable juice

1½ cups cooked veal, diced

1 can (3 or 4 ounces) sliced mushrooms

2 tablespoons parsley, finely chopped

1 tablespoon pimiento, finely chopped

1½ teaspoons onion, grated

1 teaspoon salt

¼ teaspoon poultry seasoning

Tomato wedges

Soften gelatin in ¼ cup mixed vegetable juice. Heat remaining 1¼ cups juice; add to gelatin mixture; stir until gelatin is dissolved. Combine veal, mushrooms, parsley, pimiento, onion, salt, and poultry seasoning in medium-sized bowl. Stir gelatin mixture into meat mixture. Spoon into lightly oiled loaf pan; chill until firm. Unmold on platter.

√ VEAL WITH HERB SAUCE
(Makes 4 servings)
239 calories per serving

1 tablespoon vegetable oil

1 pound veal for scallopini

2 medium-sized onions, thinly sliced

1 clove garlic, mashed

2/3 cup water

1½ tablespoons lemon juice

¾ teaspoon salt

¼ teaspoon dried oregano leaves

Heat oil in a skillet over moderately high heat (about 300 degrees); add veal slices and brown quickly on both sides. Remove veal from skillet. Reduce heat to moderate (about 250 degrees) and cook onion and garlic until tender but not brown, stirring frequently. Return veal to skillet with water, lemon juice, salt, and oregano; cover and cook over moderately low heat (about 225 degrees) 20 minutes, turning frequently, until veal is tender. Allow 3 ounces of veal and ¼ of the sauce for each serving.

BRAISED BEEF ROLL-UPS
(Makes 4 servings)
260 calories per serving

8 very thin slices beef round, about 4 inches square (about one pound)

Salt and pepper

1 green pepper, finely chopped

1 onion, finely chopped

4 stalks celery, finely chopped

¼ teaspoon poultry seasoning

Barbecue Dressing*

Preheat oven to 350 degrees.

Arrange beef slices on waxed paper; sprinkle lightly with salt and pepper. Combine green pepper, onion, celery, and poultry seasoning; toss lightly. Brush each slice of meat with Barbecue Dressing*; spread stuffing on meat slices; roll up; fasten with wooden pegs. Arrange roll-ups in shallow baking pan: add remaining stuffing and ¼ cup Barbecue Dressing.* Bake about 1½ hours. Remove wooden picks. Serve with remaining Barbecue Dressing.*

√OVEN CROQUETTES
(Makes 4 servings)
165 calories per serving of 2 croquettes

2 cups ground lean meat, cooked

1 teaspoon butter or margarine

1 tablespoon flour

Salt and pepper to taste

1 tablespoon parsley, chopped

½ cup bouillon (made with beef cube)

½ cup skim milk

2 tablespoons raw onion, chopped

2 tablespoons green pepper, chopped

1 egg

1 teaspoon Worcestershire sauce

1 tablespoon chili sauce

Preheat oven to 375 degrees.

Trim all visible fat from cooked meat; put lean meat through grinder. Melt butter; add flour and seasonings; blend well. Add bouillon and skim milk; stir and cook until slightly thickened. Add ground meat, chopped vegetables, egg, Worcestershire sauce, and chili sauce. Blend well and heat through. Use a small mold to form mixture into 8 croquettes. Place them on a lightly greased oven platter or glass pie pan. Bake about 25 minutes.

BAKED CODFISH WITH GRAPEFRUIT
(Makes 4 servings)
140 calories per serving

1 package (12 ounces) frozen codfish

1 small grapefruit

2 tablespoons grapefruit juice

2 tablespoons margarine, melted

½ teaspoon salt

⅛ teaspoon pepper

Paprika

1½ teaspoons parsley, chopped

Preheat oven to 375 degrees.

Place frozen fish in shallow baking dish. Section grapefruit; save 2 tablespoons juice. Pour grapefruit juice and melted margarine over fish. Sprinkle with salt, pepper, and paprika. Basting occasionally, bake 30 minutes or until fish flakes easily with a fork. Sprinkle grapefruit sections with paprika and arrange on top of fish; sprinkle with parsley and bake 10 minutes longer.

There's nothing depressing about dieting any-more. Because of the variety of foods available and the marvelous things you can do with them, getting to be slim can be almost fun!

✓SUKIYAKI
(Makes 6 servings)
220 calories per 2/3-cup serving

1 pound fillet of beef or boneless sirloin

¼ cup soy sauce

1 tablespoon sugar

½ cup beef broth

1 tablespoon sherry

1 cup onion, thinly sliced

1 cup bamboo shoots, sliced

1 cup celery, sliced

½ pound fresh mushrooms, thinly sliced

4 scallions with tops, cut into pieces

2 tablespoons salad oil

Have meat trimmed of all fat and cut into ⅛-inch slices. Combine soy sauce, sugar, beef broth, and sherry. Prepare vegetables. Heat oil in heavy skillet. Brown meat strips and push to side of skillet. Pour half of soy sauce mixture over meat. Add celery and onion to skillet; cook 3 minutes. Add remaining ingredients and remaining soy sauce mixture. Cook 4 minutes. Serve immediately with rice.

SKEWERED LAMB AND PINEAPPLE
(Makes 4 servings)
180 calories per serving

1 pound lean leg of lamb

½ tablespoon salad oil

¼ cup vinegar or lemon juice

½ teaspoon meat tenderizer

Salt, pepper, and garlic salt to season

Marjoram, basil, and rosemary, crushed

24 medium canned pineapple chunks, drained

Cut lamb into 24 1-inch cubes. Place in dish; sprinkle with the combined salad oil, vinegar, and meat tenderizer. Turn pieces to coat all sides. Combine seasonings and herbs; sprinkle over meat. Refrigerate at least 3 hours.

Preheat broiler. Alternate cubes of lamb and pineapple on 4 skewers. Place on broiler rack about 2 inches below heat. Broil until meat is brown, about 20 minutes, turning to brown all sides.

STUFFED GREEN PEPPERS
(Makes 4 servings)
250 calories per serving of 2 pepper halves

4 medium green peppers

1 can (1 pound) corned beef hash

1 tablespoon onion, chopped

¼ cup canned tomato puree

½ slice bread in soft bread crumbs

2 teaspoons butter or margarine

Parsley

Preheat oven to 350 degrees.

Wash the peppers, cut out stem ends, and cut in half lengthwise. Parboil peppers about 5 minutes; drain. Combine corn beef hash and onion; blend in tomato puree. Stuff the pepper halves; top with bread crumbs and dot each half pepper with ¼ teaspoon butter. Place in shallow glass baking pan, pour a little hot water around them, and bake about 25 minutes. Serve on a heated platter garnished with parsley.

LAMB CURRY
(Makes 4 servings)
228 calories per serving

1¼ pounds lean boneless lamb, cubed

½ cup onion, chopped

1 clove garlic, mashed

2 cups water

1 can (16 ounces) unsweetened applesauce

2 beef bouillon cubes

½ teaspoon salt

1¼ teaspoons curry powder

1 tablespoon cornstarch

1 tablespoon water

Place lamb, onion, garlic, the 2 cups water, applesauce, bouillon cubes, salt, and curry powder in a saucepan over moderately high heat (about 300 degrees). Cover and heat until mixture comes to a boil. Reduce heat to moderately low (about 225 degrees) and cook 1½ hours or until meat is fork-tender; add additional water if necessary. Mix the cornstarch and the 1 tablespoon water together and stir into lamb mixture; continue cooking until sauce is thickened, stirring constantly. Allow 3 ounces lamb and ¼ of the sauce per serving.

BEEF PATTIES BURGUNDY
(Makes 5 servings)
180 calories per patty

1¼ pounds lean ground round steak

1/3 cup canned, sliced mushrooms

2 tablespoons Burgundy cooking wine

Water chestnuts, thinly sliced and drained (optional)

Form ground beef into 5 patties. In heated non-stick skillet (no fat), pan-broil patties to sear in the juices. Add drained mushrooms and the Burgundy wine. Simmer slowly 15 minutes. Just before removing from heat, add water chestnuts.

CHICKEN FLORENTINE
(Makes 4 servings)
219 calories per serving

1 2½- to 3-pound broiler-fryer, quartered

Salt and pepper

1 can (4 ounces) mushroom slices

2 tablespoons Parmesan cheese, grated

¼ cup flour

A few grains of pepper

¾ teaspoon seasoned salt

1 chicken bouillon cube

1½ cups skim milk

¼ teaspoon salt

2 tablespoons low-calorie Italian-style French dressing

2 packages (10 ounces each) frozen chopped spinach, cooked

Preheat broiler.

Sprinkle chicken with salt and pepper. Place skin side down on rack in broiler pan; brush lightly with some of the French dressing. Place in broiler about 5 to 6 inches from heat. Broil 20 to 25 minutes; turn and brush with remaining dressing and meat juices from pan. Broil an additional 20 to 25 minutes or until fork-tender. While chicken is broiling, prepare sauce. Drain mushrooms and reserve liquid. In a saucepan mix flour and liquid from mushrooms. Gradually add skim milk and beat with a rotary beater to blend. Cook over moderate heat (about 250 degrees), stirring constantly, until thickened. Add the ¼ teaspoon salt, pepper, seasoned salt, and bouillon cube. Stir over moderately low heat (about 225 degrees) until bouillon cube is dissolved. Add mushrooms. Spoon well-drained cooked spinach into a heat-proof baking dish. Arrange chicken over spinach. Top with mushroom sauce and Parmesan cheese. Broil 3 to 5 minutes, 3 to 4 inches from heat.

SWISS STEAK
(Makes 4 servings)
204 calories per serving

1½ pounds chuck steak, cut ½ inch thick

Unseasoned instant meat tenderizer

Salt and pepper

1 can (16 ounces) tomatoes

1 medium-sized onion, thinly sliced

½ cup celery, chopped

½ teaspoon ground marjoram

¼ teaspoon garlic powder

¾ teaspoon salt

⅛ teaspoon pepper

Cut off all visible fat from steak. Cook pieces of fat in a heavy skillet over moderately low heat (about 225 degrees) until fat is released; discard unmelted fat. Sprinkle meat with meat tenderizer, following directions on jar; then sprinkle with salt and pepper. Brown lightly in the fat in skillet over moderately high heat (about 300 degrees). Pour off excess fat. Add remaining ingredients. Cover and cook over low heat about 2½ hours or until fork-tender. Add water during cooking if too much liquid evaporates. For diet serving, allow 3 ounces meat and ¼ of the sauce.

FILLET OF SOLE VERONIQUE
(Makes 4 servings)
291 calories per serving

1 pound fillet of sole, fresh or frozen

Salt and pepper

¼ cup dry white wine

¼ cup canned chicken broth

1½ teaspoons lemon juice

1 tablespoon butter or margarine

2 tablespoons flour

¾ cup skim milk

½ cup seedless white grapes

Preheat oven to 350 degrees.

Place fish in a shallow, lightly oiled baking dish. Sprinkle with salt and pepper. Mix together wine, chicken broth, and lemon juice and pour over fish. Cover and bake 15 minutes. While fish is baking, melt butter in a small saucepan over moderately low heat. Remove from heat and blend in flour. Gradually add skim milk and cook over moderately low heat, stirring constantly, until thickened. Remove fish from oven and drain juices from baking dish into cream sauce, stirring until blended. Pour sauce over fish and sprinkle with grapes. Place in preheated broiler about 4 inches from heat for about 5 minutes or until sauce starts to brown.

TROPICAL CHICKEN
(Makes 4 servings)
360 calories per serving

1 cup orange juice

¾ cup (8¾-ounce can) crushed pineapple, drained

¼ cup brown sugar, firmly packed

3½-to 4-pound chicken, quartered

Preheat oven to 375 degrees.

Combine orange juice, crushed pineapple, and brown sugar. Place chicken pieces in a baking pan and pour orange-pineapple mixture over the chicken. Bake about 1 hour, 15 minutes or until done. Baste chicken with the sauce while cooking.

Buy an inexpensive belt and punch additional notches about one-half inch apart. It's easier than using a tape measure to keep track of your shrinking waistline.

CREOLE SHRIMP
(Makes 6 servings)
360 calories per serving

2 tablespoons butter or margarine

1 medium onion, thinly sliced

1 small green pepper, sliced

½ cup celery, chopped

1 small clove garlic, minced

3 tablespoons flour

1½ cups water

2 cans (8-ounces each) tomato sauce

1 bay leaf

2 teaspoons salt

½ teaspoon oregano

½ teaspoon chili powder

2 pounds raw shrimp

Melt butter or margarine in a deep heavy pot. Add onion, green pepper, celery, and garlic; saute until tender. In a small cup combine flour and water; stir into pot along with tomato sauce, bay leaf, salt, oregano, and chili powder. Bring to a boil; simmer about 20 minutes. Add shrimp. Cook mixture uncovered until shrimp is pink. Serve with rice.

✓SALMON LOAF WITH MUSHROOM SAUCE
(Makes 4 servings)
340 calories per serving

2 cups (1-pound can) canned salmon, drained and flaked

2/3 cup liquid (drained salmon liquid with water added)

1 cup dry bread crumbs

¼ cup ripe olives, pitted and chopped

1 egg

1 tablespoon lemon juice

½ teaspoon salt

⅛ teaspoon pepper

Preheat oven to 375 degrees.

Mix all ingredients together until well blended. Turn into greased 9 x 5 x 3-inch pan. Bake about 45 minutes or until done. Let stand a few minutes. Loosen edges with spatula and unmold on serving platter. Serve hot with Mushroom Sauce.*

MUSHROOM SAUCE

1 cup liquid (drained mushroom liquid with water added)

1/3 cup instant nonfat dry milk solids

2 tablespoons flour

½ teaspoon salt

Pinch of pepper

¾ cup (4-ounce can) canned sliced mushrooms, drained

In saucepan combine drained mushroom liquid and water mixture with dry milk solids, flour, salt, and pepper. Beat with rotary beater until well blended. Cook over medium heat, stirring constantly, until sauce thickens and comes to a boil. Remove from heat. Stir in mushrooms. Serve with Salmon Loaf.*

CHICKEN A L'ORANGE
(Makes 4 servings)
340 calories per serving

½ cup flour

1 tablespoon salt

2 teaspoons orange peel, grated

1 teaspoon paprika

¼ teaspoon pepper

1 2½-to 3-pound fryer, cut up

1 tablespoon butter or margarine

¼ cup water

2 cups orange juice

2 tablespoons brown sugar

1 teaspoon salt

¼ teaspoon ground ginger

⅛ teaspoon cinnamon

Combine flour, salt, orange peel, paprika, and pepper in a bag. Drop in chicken pieces and toss until well coated with flour. Reserve 2 tablespoons of flour mixture.

Melt butter or margarine in skillet. Cook chicken over low heat until brown on all sides. Add water; cover and simmer gently 30 minutes or until tender. Turn occasionally and add more water if necessary. Remove chicken to warm platter. Pour off pan drippings, reserving 2 tablespoons. Return to skillet with 2 tablespoons of reserved flour mixture. Blend well. Combine remaining ingredients and add gradually to skillet, stirring constantly; cook until mixture boils. Serve over chicken.

CHICKEN JAMBALAYA
(Makes 6 servings)
250 calories per serving

2 tablespoons butter or margarine

1 cup rice

1 cup celery, sliced

½ cup onion, finely chopped

1 clove garlic, finely chopped

1 cup water

1 beef bouillon cube

3½ cups (2 14½-ounce cans) stewed tomatoes

2 cups cooked chicken, cubed

7 ounces shelled, cleaned shrimp

1 cup (7½-ounce can) minced clams

1 cup canned or frozen peas, cooked

1 bay leaf

1 teaspoon salt

⅛ teaspoon pepper

Preheat oven to 375 degrees.

Melt butter or margarine in large skillet. Add rice, celery, onion, and garlic. Saute until rice is light brown and vegetables tender. Add tomatoes, water, and bouillon cube. Cover and cook 15 to 20 minutes or until rice is tender.

Combine rice mixture with remaining ingredients in 3-quart casserole. Bake, covered, 30 minutes.

FISH PIE
(Makes 6 servings)
280 calories per serving

1½ pounds frozen fish fillets, thawed

10 small cooked onions, sliced

1 tablespoon pimiento, thinly sliced

1/3 cup green pepper, chopped

3 tablespoons butter or margarine

4 tablespoons flour

4 cups mashed potatoes (prepared with skim milk)

Paprika

1 cup skim milk

2 tablespoons lemon juice

1½ teaspoons salt

½ teaspoon Worcestershire sauce

¼ teaspoon pepper

Preheat oven to 425 degrees.

Poach the fish until done; strain and reserve 1 cup stock. Alternate layers of fish, onion, and pimiento in a 2½-quart casserole. Saute green pepper in butter or margarine for 5 minutes. Blend in flour; slowly stir in milk and reserved fish stock. Cook, stirring until sauce thickens and begins to bubble. Add lemon juice, salt, Worcestershire sauce, and pepper. Pour sauce over fish in dish. Top with mashed potatoes. Sprinkle with paprika. Bake 25 to 30 minutes or until heated through and browned.

MEATBALLS IN TOMATO SAUCE
(Makes 4 servings)
335 calories per serving

3 slices enriched white bread

1¼ cups tomato juice

1 pound ground beef

½ cup onion, chopped

1 egg, slightly beaten

¾ teaspoon salt

½ teaspoon poultry seasoning

¼ teaspoon paprika

Soak bread in tomato juice; squeeze out excess juice and save. Crumble bread: add to meat. Blend in onion, egg, and seasonings; shape into small balls (about 1 inch in diameter). Heat tomato sauce in skillet; add meatballs. Simmer, covered, until meatballs are done, about 25 minutes.

There's a lot of flavor in one link sausage if you eat it very slowly.

CHICKEN POT PIE
(Makes 6 servings)
335 calories per serving

1½ cups water

½ cup instant nonfat dry milk solids

3 tablespoons flour

1 teaspoon salt

¼ teaspoon tarragon

¼ teaspoon parsley

⅛ teaspoon pepper

3 cups cooked, boned chicken, cubed

¾ cup (8-ounce can) white onions, cooked

½ cup carrot slices, cooked

½ cup lima beans, cooked

½ cup peas, cooked

½ cup flour

⅛ teaspoon salt

2 tablespoons butter or margarine

2 tablespoons water

Preheat oven to 400 degrees.

Combine water, milk solids, 3 tablespoons flour, 1 teaspoon salt, tarragon, parsley, and pepper. Beat until smooth. Cook over medium heat, stirring constantly, until mixture comes to a boil. Fold in chicken, onions, carrots, beans, and peas. Pour into a 1½-quart casserole.

Combine ½ cup flour and salt. Cut in butter or margarine with pastry blender or two knives. Add water and blend in with fork. Roll out to cover casserole. Place over casserole; pinch edges firmly to edge of casserole. Prick pastry top with fork. Bake 20 minutes.

TANGY BARBECUE CHICKEN
(Makes about 5 servings)
235 calories per serving

1 3-pound fryer, cut up

2/3 cup catsup

1/3 cup hot water

2 tablespoons onion, chopped

2 tablespoons lemon juice

2 tablespoons vegetable oil

1 teaspoon Worcestershire sauce

1 teaspoon sugar

¼ teaspoon chili powder

Preheat broiler.

Place chicken on broiler pan. Combine remaining ingredients; brush chicken. Broil about 35 to 40 minutes or until done, frequently basting with sauce on all sides until sauce is used.

CRABMEAT BOUILLABAISSE
(Makes 10 servings)
200 calories per serving

2 cups (3 medium) onions, sliced

2 tablespoons margarine

2 cups celery, diced

2 cups raw potatoes, diced

2 green peppers, cut into strips

2½ teaspoons salt

1 bay leaf

1 teaspoon garlic, minced

1 pound shrimp, cleaned

1 pound scallops

1 teaspoon basil

Pepper to taste

4 cups boiling water

¾ cup (7-ounce can) tomato paste

1½ cups (6½-ounce can) crabmeat, broken into pieces

In a deep pot, saute onion in margarine until lightly browned. Add celery, potatoes, green pepper, salt, bay leaf, garlic, basil, and pepper to taste. Pour in boiling water; cover and simmer 20 minutes. Blend in tomato paste; add crabmeat, shrimp, and scallops. Cover; simmer 15 minutes longer. Serve in deep soup bowls.

TUNA RING
(Makes 5 servings)
250 calories per serving

1 cup (2 7-ounce cans) water-packed tuna

2 tablespoons onion, finely chopped

2 tablespoons green pepper, finely chopped

2 tablespoons pimiento, finely chopped

2 teaspoons Worcestershire sauce

1 teaspoon salt

⅛ teaspoon pepper

1 cup water

¾ cup dry bread crumbs

½ cup peas, cooked

1/3 cup nonfat dry milk solids

¼ cup slivered almonds

1 egg

Preheat oven to 350 degrees.

Combine all ingredients. Spoon into well-greased 8-inch ring mold. Bake 45 minutes. Turn out at once.

SALMON BAKED IN FOIL
(Makes 8 servings)
315 calories per serving

1 cup water

½ cup onion, chopped

¼ cup lemon juice

½ teaspoon basil

¼ teaspoon tarragon

¼ teaspoon rosemary

½ teaspoon salt

2 lemon slices

3 pounds salmon steaks

2 tablespoons flour

Preheat oven to 375 degrees.

Combine water, onion, lemon juice, spices, and lemon slices in a saucepan. Simmer gently 20 minutes. Meanwhile, wash and dry salmon steaks and place on a long sheet of foil, bringing up the edges around the fish. Pour the sauce mixture over the fish and completely enclose the fish, crimping the foil to seal the edges tightly. Place the foil-wrapped fish in a baking pan. Bake 30 to 45 minutes or until the fish flakes easily with a fork. Remove fish to a platter and pour remaining juices into a saucepan. Add flour and cook over medium heat until thickened. Pour over fish. Serve.

DIETER'S BEEF STROGANOFF
(Makes 5 servings)
240 calories per individual serving

1 pound raw beef tenderloin

2 tablespoons butter or margarine

½ pound fresh mushrooms, sliced

½ cup onion, chopped

1 can (10½ ounces) condensed beef bouillon

½ cup buttermilk

2 tablespoons flour

Salt and pepper to taste

Have beef tenderloin trimmed of fat and sliced ¼ inch thick. Cut into strips ¼ inch wide. Brown quickly in butter in skillet; push meat to one side. Add mushrooms and onion; cook until tender, but not brown. Add condensed beef bouillon; heat just to boiling. Blend buttermilk with flour; stir into bouillon. Cook, stirring constantly until thickened (sauce will be relatively thin). Add salt and pepper. Serve over rice. Makes 3 cups.

PEAS SUPERB
(Makes 5 servings)
110 calories per serving

2½ cups fresh peas (about 2 pounds unshelled)

1 tablespoon butter or margarine

1 cup fresh mushrooms, sliced

2 tablespoons onion, chopped

Cook peas in salted water until tender. Melt butter or margarine in skillet. Saute mushrooms and onions. Stir in drained peas.

SOUTHERN GREEN BEANS
(Makes 4 servings)
65 calories per serving

1 pound fresh green beans, cooked

2 cups (1-pound can) tomatoes

½ cup celery, chopped

¼ cup green pepper, chopped

¼ teaspoon onion salt

Combine green beans, tomatoes, celery, green pepper, and onion salt. Cook over medium heat about 15 minutes or until well heated.

SWISS LUNCHEON CUSTARD
(Makes 4 servings)
268 calories per serving

4 egg yolks

1 1/3 cups skim milk

1½ cups Swiss cheese, coarsely shredded

½ teaspoon prepared mustard

⅛ teaspoon Worcestershire sauce

¼ teaspoon salt

4 egg whites, stiffly beaten

Preheat oven to 350 degrees.

Beat egg yolks well with a rotary beater; add skim milk, cheese, mustard, Worcestershire sauce, and salt. Fold in stiffly beaten egg whites. Pour into 4 greased 10-ounce pie dishes (about 1¾ inches deep). Place in a large baking pan; add 1 inch warm water to pan. Bake 40 minutes or until custard is just set in the center.

PARSLEY RICE
(Makes 4 servings)
140 calories per serving

½ cup rice

1 cup cold water

¼ cup onion, minced

½ teaspoon salt

2 tablespoons butter or margarine

¼ cup parsley, minced

Combine rice, cold water, onion, and salt in saucepan. Cover and bring to a boil over high heat. Reduce heat and simmer slowly until all liquid is absorbed. about 12 to 15 minutes. Stir in butter or margarine and parsley.

DEVILED BEETS
(Makes 4 servings)
90 calories per serving

2 1/3 cups whole beets, cooked

1 tablespoon butter or margarine

1 tablespoon honey

1 teaspoon salt

½ teaspoon Worcestershire sauce

Drain liquid from beets and combine liquid with butter or margarine, honey, salt, and Worcestershire sauce. Bring to a boil and simmer 15 minutes. Add beets and cook 10 minutes or until beets are hot and most of liquid is reduced.

LIMA BEANS WITH HERBS
(Makes 4 servings)
120 calories per serving

1 package (10 ounces) frozen lima beans

1 cup celery, diced

¼ cup onion, chopped

1 tablespoon butter or margarine

1 teaspoon sweet basil

½ teaspoon salt

Cook lima beans as directed on the package. Drain. Saute celery and onion in butter or margarine until tender. Blend in sweet basil and salt. Add the cooked lima beans and toss gently. Continue cooking until thoroughly heated.

HOT POTATO SALAD
(Makes 8 servings)
60 calories per serving

4 baking potatoes

1 tablespoon vegetable oil

¼ cup onion, minced

3 tablespoons vinegar

1½ teaspoons sugar

1 teaspoon salt

2 tablespoons green pepper, chopped

1 tablespoon pimiento, chopped

Preheat oven to 400 degrees.

Bake potatoes about 1 hour or until done. Place 1 tablespoon vegetable oil in small skillet; add onions and saute until tender. Stir in vinegar, sugar, and salt. Continue cooking until mixture is hot; remove from heat. When potatoes are baked, cut in half and scoop out centers; reserve potato shells. Beat together potatoes and hot onion-vinegar mixture. Blend in green pepper and pimiento. Spoon potato mixture back into shells. Place under broiler for about 5 minutes or until lightly browned.

CURRIED MIXED VEGETABLES
(Makes 6 servings)
65 calories per serving

1½ cups water

½ cup instant nonfat dry milk solids

3 tablespoons flour

1 teaspoon salt

¼ to ½ teaspoon curry powder

⅛ teaspoon pepper

4 cups mixed vegetables (string beans, carrots, cauliflower, onions, etc.), cooked

Pour water into a saucepan. Sprinkle the dry milk, flour, salt, curry powder, and pepper evenly over water. Beat with rotary beater until well blended. Cook over medium heat, stirring constantly, until sauce thickens. Add mixed vegetables to sauce and continue cooking until vegetables are heated through. Pour into serving dish.

LEMON-CHIVE ASPARAGUS SPEARS
(Makes about 3 servings)
70 calories per serving

1 pound (about 12 spears) fresh, or 1 package (10 ounces) frozen, asparagus spears

3 tablespoons fine bread crumbs   1 teaspoon lemon peel, grated

1 tablespoon chives, chopped   ¼ teaspoon salt

2 teaspoons butter or margarine

Cook asparagus spears until tender. Combine bread crumbs, chives, butter or margarine, lemon peel, and salt. Place hot cooked asparagus spears on serving dish; sprinkle with crumb mixture.

Buy cartons of low-calorie carbonated drinks.

BROCCOLI WITH MUSTARD DILL SAUCE
(Makes 4 servings)
80 calories per serving

4 teaspoons prepared mustard

1 teaspoon salt

¼ teaspoon dill seed

1 cup water

1/3 cup instant nonfat dry milk solids

3 tablespoons flour

1 package (10 ounces) frozen broccoli spears, cooked

In a saucepan combine water, instant nonfat dry milk, flour, prepared mustard, salt, and dill seed. Beat with rotary beater until well blended. Cook over medium heat, stirring constantly, until sauce thickens. Pour over broccoli spears and serve.

GLAZED ONIONS
(Makes 4 servings)
110 calories per serving

2 tablespoons water

2 tablespoons dark brown sugar

1 tablespoon butter or margarine

3 cups (2 15½-ounce cans) peeled whole white onions, drained

In a skillet, combine water, brown sugar, and butter or margarine. Heat until sugar and margarine have melted. Add drained onions and simmer, stirring occasionally, until golden brown.

OVEN FRENCH FRIES
(Makes 4 servings)
100 calories per 1/2 cup serving

3 medium raw potatoes

1 tablespoon salad oil

1 tablespoon water

Salt to taste

Preheat oven to 425 degrees.

Cut raw potatoes into strips. Mix oil and water in bowl; add potato strips and mix until coated with mixture. Place in shallow pan. Bake 45 minutes to 1 hour. Salt lightly and serve hot. Raw potatoes may be prepared shoestring style.

ORIENTAL CAULIFLOWER
(Makes 5 servings)
80 calories per serving

1 large head cauliflower

¼ cup sugar

2 tablespoons cornstarch

¼ teaspoon salt

¼ teaspoon monosodium glutamate

1 can (8¾ ounces) pineapple tidbits

¼ cup vinegar

Paprika

Cook cauliflower in lightly salted water until tender. Drain and keep warm. Combine sugar, cornstarch, salt, and monosodium glutamate in a saucepan. Drain pineapple tidbits. Add enough water to the pineapple syrup to make 2/3 cup liquid. Blend pineapple liquid into dry ingredients. Add vinegar and then the pineapple tidbits. Cook over medium heat, stirring constantly, until mixture thickens, becomes clear, and begins to boil. Place cauliflower in serving dish. Pour over the sauce and sprinkle with paprika.

√ BAKED MASHED SQUASH
(Makes 6 servings)
80 calories per serving

3 cups cooked squash (acorn, butternut), mashed

¼ cup orange juice

1½ teaspoons salt

1 teaspoon orange peel, grated

⅛ teaspoon pepper

⅛ teaspoon cinnamon

¼ cup dark brown sugar, firmly packed

Preheat oven to 375 degrees.

Combine all ingredients except brown sugar. Blend well. Place in a 1-quart casserole and sprinkle the top evenly with brown sugar. Bake 20 minutes.

CREOLE CELERY
(Makes 4 servings)
55 calories per serving

1 tablespoon butter or margarine

2 cups celery, sliced

¼ cup onion, chopped

1½ cups (1-pound, 3-ounce can) tomatoes, drained

⅛ teaspoon pepper

¾ teaspoon salt

2 tablespoons parsley, chopped

Melt butter or margarine in a saucepan. Add celery, onion, salt, and pepper. Simmer, covered, 10 minutes. Add tomatoes. Continue to cook, covered, 5 minutes or until celery is done and tomatoes are hot. Add parsley.

CARROTS AND MUSHROOMS
(Makes 4 servings)
35 calories per 1/2-cup serving

2 cups carrots, sliced

½ teaspoon salt

1 can (3 ounces) sliced mushrooms with liquid

Dash of pepper

⅛ to ¼ teaspoon ginger

Slice carrots into saucepan; sprinkle with salt, pepper, and ginger. Add mushrooms, including the liquid (but not any added fat). Cover tightly; bring to boil. Cook gently until just tender, from 5 to 10 minutes.

√ SAVORY GREEN BEANS
(Makes 6 servings)
65 calories per serving

1 pound green beans

2 tablespoons butter or margarine

½ cup onion, finely chopped

¼ teaspoon combined rosemary, basil, and thyme

¼ cup celery, chopped

¼ cup parsley, chopped

¾ teaspoon salt

Wash beans, cross cut, and cook until tender. Melt butter or margarine in a saucepan. Add onion and celery; saute 5 minutes. Mix in parsley and seasonings. Simmer, covered, 10 minutes or until tender. Toss with beans.

DR. PAGE'S DELIGHT SALAD DRESSING
3 calories per tablespoon

½ cup cider vinegar   ½ teaspoon salt

¼ teaspoon paprika   1 clove garlic, grated

½ grain saccharin   1 tablespoon onion, grated

Shake all ingredients in a closed jar or beat well. Shake before each use.

Make a practice of studying the calorie count in the low-cal food section. New products appear frequently.

✓ SCALLOPED POTATOES
(Makes 8 servings)
125 calories per serving

2 cups water

2/3 cup instant nonfat dry milk solids

4 tablespoons flour

1 teaspoon salt

⅛ teaspoon pepper

4 cups potatoes, thinly sliced

½ cup onion, chopped

Preheat oven to 375 degrees.

Combine water, dry milk, flour, salt, and pepper in a saucepan. Beat with rotary beater until well blended. Cook over medium heat, stirring constantly, until sauce thickens and boils. Remove from heat. Place 2 cups of potatoes in a 1½-quart casserole. Sprinkle with half the onion and pour on half the sauce. Layer the remaining 2 cups of potatoes, onion, and sauce. Bake 1 hour or until potatoes are tender.

✓ PARSLEY CARROTS AND POTATOES
(Makes 6 servings)
105 calories per serving

1½ teaspoons salt

1 cup water

2 cups carrots, thinly sliced and pared

2 cups potatoes, thinly sliced and pared

¼ cup onion, minced

2 tablespoons butter or margarine

½ cup parsley, chopped or snipped

1 teaspoon caraway seeds (optional)

⅛ teaspoon pepper

Bring salted water to a boil in saucepan. Add carrots, potatoes, and onion. Cover and cook until tender, about 10 minutes. Drain. Lightly toss in butter or margarine, parsley, caraway seeds, and pepper until blended.

SPICED BEETS
(Makes 6 servings)
30 calories per 1/3-cup serving

1 can (1 pound) beets

1 tablespoon onion, chopped

½ teaspoon salt

⅛ teaspoon ground cloves

⅛ teaspoon nutmeg

1 dash pepper

1 teaspoon sugar

¾ cup beet liquor

3 tablespoons lemon juice

Drain canned beets; slice or dice. Add the chopped onion, salt, spices, pepper, and sugar to the beet liquor; heat to boiling. Add lemon juice and pour over the beets. Serve hot or cold.

✓ BAKED ACORN SQUASH
(Makes 4 servings)
75 calories per serving of 1/2 squash

2 medium acorn squash

1 tablespoon butter or margarine

Nutmeg

Salt and pepper to taste

Preheat oven to 400 degrees.

Scrub acorn squash. Cut in half lengthwise, scrape out seeds and stringy portion. Place cut side down in lightly greased baking pan. Bake 45 minutes. Remove from oven. Brush inside of squash halves with melted butter; add seasonings. Return to oven and bake 15 minutes longer.

Other herbs that may be used are Season-All and basil leaves. For a gourmet touch, add 2 slivered filberts for the last 15 minutes of baking.

DIETER'S MAYONNAISE
(Makes about 1-3/4 cup)
15 calories per 1-tablespoon serving

1 tablespoon flour

2 tablespoons sugar

1¼ teaspoon salt

Pinch of red pepper

1 teaspoon prepared mustard

1 tablespoon salad oil

1 cup water

2 medium eggs

4 tablespoons vinegar

Blend together flour, sugar, salt, red pepper, prepared mustard, salad oil, and water in top of double boiler. Cook over hot water, stirring constantly, until slightly thickened.

In another bowl, beat eggs slightly, then gradually add the vinegar. Slowly add half of the hot sauce to the egg and vinegar. Put it into the double boiler and cook it over hot but not boiling water until mixture coats a spoon. Be careful not to overcook the eggs or dressing will curdle. Remove from heat and pour into jar. When cool, cover and refrigerate.

VARIATIONS

To make Russian dressing, add 1 tablespoon catsup to ¼ cup Dieter's Mayonnaise.* One tablespoon of Russian dressing is 16 calories.

For gourmet dressing, add ½ teaspoon horseradish and a dash of Worcestershire sauce to ¼ cup Russian dressing. One tablespoon of gourmet dressing is 16 calories.

For Thousand Island dressing, add 2 tablespoons chili sauce, 2 tablespoons chopped green pepper and ½ hard-cooked, chopped egg to ½ cup Dieter's Mayonnaise.* One and a half tablespoons dressing is 22 calories.

DR. PAGE'S FRUIT SALAD DRESSING
6 calories per tablespoon

1 clove garlic, minced

¼ cup cider vinegar

½ cup orange juice, unstrained

¼ teaspoon paprika

1 grain saccharin

½ teaspoon each of salt and pepper

Let garlic stand in vinegar for 1 hour. Strain. Add the rest of the ingredients, altering saccharin content to taste. Shake in a closed jar or beat well. Chill. Shake before each use.

Don't buy "sinful" foods such as cakes, cookies or other items that are not on the list. If they're not in the house, the dieter won't be lured by them.

LEMON-CAPER SAUCE
(Makes about 1/3 cup)
Zero calories

¼ teaspoon flour

1 tablespoon water

3 tablespoons lemon juice

6 drops liquid no-calorie sweetener

2 tablespoons capers, drained

1 teaspoon prepared horseradish

Blend flour and water in small saucepan; add lemon juice and sweetener. Cook over low heat, stirring constantly, until sauce thickens and boils 1 minute. Stir in capers and horseradish. Serve hot or cold with seafood.

FRENCH DRESSING
(Makes about 1/2 cup)
50 calories per tablespoon

5 tablespoons salad oil

4 tablespoons vinegar

¼ teaspoon salt

¼ teaspoon paprika

¼ teaspoon dry mustard

¼ teaspoon liquid no-calorie sweetener

1 clove of garlic

Combine all ingredients in small jar with screw top; shake well. Chill to blend flavors. Remove garlic; shake well before using.

DIET SOUR CREAM
20 calories per tablespoon

Allow ½ pint of half-and-half to reach room temperature. Stir in 1 to 2 tablespoons lemon juice or mild vinegar. When "soured," store in refrigerator. Use within one week.

TOMATO JUICE DRESSING
(Makes about 3/4 cup)
Zero calories

½ cup tomato juice

2 tablespoons lemon juice

1 teaspoon onion, grated

½ teaspoon dry mustard

½ teaspoon Worcestershire sauce

Combine all ingredients in jar with screw top; shake well. Chill to blend flavors. Shake well before using. Serve on vegetable salads.

TANGY SEAFOOD COCKTAIL SAUCE
(Makes about 1/2 cup)
Zero calories

½ cup tomato juice

1 teaspoon prepared horseradish

1 teaspoon lemon juice

½ teaspoon Worcestershire sauce

½ teaspoon parsley, finely chopped

½ teaspoon salt

Combine all ingredients; chill to blend flavors.

NO-CALORIE FRUIT DRESSING
(Makes about 1 cup)
Zero calories

4 tablespoons vinegar

2 tablespoons water

1 clove garlic, sliced

¼ teaspoon salt

⅛ teaspoon paprika

¼ teaspoon liquid no-calorie sweetener

1 tablespoon chives (optional)

Combine all ingredients in measuring cup; chill. Use to marinate cooked vegetables or a mixed green salad.

LEMON FRUIT DRESSING
(Makes about 1 cup)
55 calories per 1-tablespoon serving

½ cup undiluted frozen lemonade concentrate

1/3 cup honey

2 tablespoons vegetable oil

1 teaspoon poppy seeds (optional)

Combine all ingredients in small bowl. Beat with rotary beater until smooth.

VINEGAR DRESSING
(Makes about 1/3 cup)
Zero calories

1 teaspoon unflavored gelatin

¾ cup orange juice

5 tablespoons lemon juice

½ teaspoon liquid no-calorie sweetener

¼ teaspoon salt

¼ teaspoon paprika

Pepper

Soften gelatin in ¼ cup orange juice in small bowl. Heat remaining orange juice; pour over gelatin to dissolve; add remaining ingredients; chill until syrupy. Beat with rotary beater until fluffy.

MINT SAUCE

Combine 2 tablespoons water, ½ cup vinegar, ½ teaspoon liquid no-calorie sweetener, and the leaves from 1 dozen sprigs of fresh mint (finely chopped). Let stand in warm place for about an hour.

PEACHES IN SHERRY
(Makes 4 servings)
88 calories per serving

1 can (16 ounces) water-packed peach halves

2 tablespoons sherry

¼ teaspoon ground cinnamon

⅛ teaspoon ground nutmeg

¼ cup toasted flaked coconut

Drain peaches, reserving juice. Mix together juice, sherry, cinnamon, and nutmeg. Pour over peaches and chill. Serve garnished with coconut.

Eggs may be prepared in any form. Even fried eggs can be cooked in a no-stick pan, using no fat. Hard-boiled eggs provide the best and longest reprieve from hunger. Scrambled eggs are the next best method.

BARBECUE DRESSING
(Makes 1-1/2 cups)
Zero calories

½ cup tomato catsup

½ teaspoon salt

½ teaspoon dry mustard

½ teaspoon liquid no-calorie sweetener

Dash of chili powder

Dash of liquid pepper seasoning

1 cup water

Mix catsup, salt, mustard, sweetener, chili powder, and liquid pepper seasoning in small bowl; gradually stir in water.

SPICED VINEGAR
(Makes 1 pint)
Zero calories

2 cups vinegar

1 teaspoon liquid no-calorie sweetener

¼ teaspoon peppercorns

½ teaspoon whole cloves

½ teaspoon allspice

½ teaspoon celery seeds

½ teaspoon mustard seeds

½ teaspoon tumeric

½ teaspoon ginger

½ teaspoon mace

Combine all ingredients in quart jar with screw top; let stand 2 weeks, shaking well each day. Strain through 4 thicknesses of cheesecloth; store in same jar.

CRANBERRY-ORANGE RELISH

Put through food chopper with coarse plate, 1 cup washed fresh cranberries and ½ unpeeled orange with seeds removed. Stir in 1 teaspoon no-calorie sweetener.

SKIM MILK CUSTARD
(Makes 4 servings)
135 calories per serving

2/3 cup dry powdered skim milk

Warm water

2 eggs

¼ cup sugar

1 teaspoon vanilla extract

¼ teaspoon powdered nutmeg

Preheat oven to 350 degrees.

Blend together dry powdered skim milk and 1 cup warm water. Add more water to bring the volume to 2 cups. Beat in eggs, sugar, vanilla extract and nutmeg, using rotary beater or blender. Lightly grease 4 6-ounce custard cups around rim *only*. Divide mixture evenly between the 4 cups. Set them in a pan containing 1 inch hot water. Bake 45 minutes or until knife blade inserted into the custard comes out clean.

MELON RING WITH RASPBERRIES
(Makes 3 servings)
85 calories per serving

1 cantaloupe, cut into 3 1-inch-thick rings

1 cup fresh red raspberries

Wash and dry melon; refrigerate in plastic or paper bag. Prepare raspberries; chill. At serving time cut melon into rings; remove seeds and membrane; peel rings. Place each ring on serving plate; fill center with ¼ cup fresh red raspberries.

CUSTARD SAUCE
(Makes 3/4 cup)
15 calories per tablespoon

¾ cup skim milk

2 egg yolks, slightly beaten

1 teaspoon liquid no-calorie sweetener

Dash of salt

½ teaspoon vanilla

Combine milk, egg yolks, sweetener, and salt in top of double boiler; cook over simmering water, stirring constantly, about 6 minutes or until mixture thickens and coats spoon. Remove from heat; add vanilla; chill.

SPANISH CREAM
(Makes 3 servings)
50 calories per serving

1½ teaspoons unflavored gelatin

1 cup skim milk

1 egg yolk, slightly beaten

Dash of salt

½ teaspoon liquid no-calorie sweetener

½ teaspoon vanilla

1 egg white, stiffly beaten

Soften gelatin in milk in top of double boiler 5 minutes; heat over boiling water until gelatin is dissolved. Gradually pour gelatin mixture over egg yolk, stirring constantly; add salt and sweetener. Return to double boiler; cook over simmering water, stirring constantly, about 5 minutes or until mixture coats spoon; add vanilla; chill until syrupy. Fold in egg white; pour into 3 individual molds, 2/3 cup size; chill until set. Serve plain or garnished with fruit.

BROILED GRAPEFRUIT
(Makes 2 servings)
85 calories per serving

1 medium-sized pink grapefruit, heavy with juice   1 tablespoon brown sugar

Preheat broiler.

Halve grapefruit and remove seeds. Loosen pulp from membrane by running a very sharp knife completely around each section, without cutting into the white membrane. Place grapefruit halves on shallow pan on broiler rack. Top with brown sugar. Broil slowly (from 3 to 4 inches under heat) until sugar is melted, the grapefruit heated through, and the edges lightly browned, 20 minutes or more. Serve hot.

MELON BALL FRUIT CUP
(Makes 1 serving)
50 calories per serving

¼ cup (3 or 4) honeydew melon balls

½ cup cantaloupe balls

⅛ cup blueberries

Mint sprig

Combine chilled melon balls in serving cup; sprinkle with blueberries. Garnish with mint sprig.

CAFE AU LAIT
(Makes 1 serving)
120 calories per serving

¾ cup boiling water

2 teaspoons freeze-dried coffee

2 saccharin tablets (or liquid artificial sweetener)

½ cup dry powdered skim milk

¼ cup warm water

Dissolve dry powdered skim milk in warm water. Add boiling water. Stir in freeze-dried coffee and saccharin or liquid artificial sweetener.

MAPLE ROYAL
(Makes 4 servings)
110 calories per serving

1 package Custard Flavor Dessert

2¼ cups skim milk

¼ teaspoon maple flavoring

Empty Custard Flavor Dessert into a saucepan. Stir in milk and maple flavoring. Cook over medium heat to a full boil, stirring occasionally. Remove from heat. (Mixture will be thin; it thickens as it cools.) Pour into heat-proof dessert dishes. Chill without stirring.

FROZEN PLUM CREME
(Makes 6 servings)
145 calories per serving

1 can (16 ounces) purple plums, drained

1 package (2 ounces) whipped topping mix

½ cup cold milk

3 tablespoons sugar

1 teaspoon lemon juice

Vanilla-wafer crumbs (optional)

Prepare about 3 hours before serving or early in the day.

Peel plums and remove pits. Blend plums until smooth in covered electric blender container at high speed; set aside. In small bowl, with mixer at high speed, beat whipped topping mix with milk until soft peaks form. Reduce speed to low; add pureed plums, sugar, and lemon juice and beat 2 minutes. Line 6 2¾-inch muffin cups with paper liners; spoon in mixture. Sprinkle tops with vanilla-wafer crumbs if desired. Freeze 2 to 3 hours or until firm.

APRICOT FLUFF
(Makes 6 servings)
40 calories per serving

1 can (1 pound, 4 ounces) low-calorie-pack apricots

1 envelope unflavored gelatin

1 teaspoon liquid no-calorie sweetener

Dash of salt

2 egg whites

Drain apricots, saving liquid; press fruit through sieve; set aside. Soften gelatin in ¼ cup apricot juice. Heat remaining juice; stir in gelatin to dissolve. Add apricot puree (save ¼ cup pulp to spoon over dessert, if desired), sweetener, and salt. Chill until syrupy. Beat egg whites until stiff but not dry; beat syrupy mixture until fluffy; fold into egg whites. Spoon into mold; chill until stiff. Serve with or without Custard Sauce.*

PINEAPPLE-MINT SHERBET
(Makes 6 servings)
45 calories per serving

2 teaspoons unflavored gelatin

1½ cups pineapple juice

2 tablespoons nonfat dry-milk powder

Dash of salt

1½ teaspoons liquid no-calorie sweetener

⅛ teaspoon peppermint extract

2 egg whites, stiffly beaten

Soften gelatin in ¼ cup cold pineapple juice, saving rest of juice. Mix milk powder and salt with enough of remaining pineapple juice to moisten in top of double boiler; add rest of juice very slowly, stirring constantly to prevent lumping. Heat milk-pineapple mixture over simmering water until hot; add softened gelatin; stir until dissolved, remove from heat; add peppermint and sweetener. Pour into freezer tray; chill until syrupy. Scrape into medium-sized bowl; beat with rotary beater until fluffy; fold in egg whites; return to tray; chill until firm, stirring occasionally. Serve garnished with fresh mint, if desired.

Concentrate on chicken and fish for main courses. If you use lamb or beef, the portions must be small and very lean. Remember, a big juicy Porterhouse steak (1 pound) means 1,600 calories where 1 pound of filet of sole has 360. And if you like chicken, a 1-pound broiler has 380!

CRANBERRY JELLY
(Makes 5 servings)
25 calories per serving

2 cups fresh cranberries

¾ cup water

2 teaspoons liquid no-calorie sweetener

1½ teaspoons unflavored gelatin

2 tablespoons cold water

Combine cranberries, ¾ cup water, and sweetener in medium-sized saucepan; simmer gently about 10 minutes or until cranberries pop open. Soften gelatin in 2 tablespoons cold water; dissolve in hot cranberry mixture; pour into individual molds. Chill until firm.

✓ DOUBLE APRICOT SOUFFLE
(Makes 6 servings)
63 calories per serving

1 can (1 pound) low-calorie apricot halves

2 packages unflavored gelatin

2 cans (12 ounces each) low-calorie apricot nectar

Juice of 1 lemon

4 egg whites, stiffly beaten

Drain apricots and stir juice into gelatin; let stand for 5 minutes, then stir over low heat until gelatin dissolves. Stir in apricot nectar and lemon juice. Chill until slightly thickened. Fold in egg whites. Dice apricots and fold in. Pour mixture into a 1½-quart souffle dish. Chill until firm.

✓ GRAPE GELATIN
(Makes 6 servings)
25 calories per serving

1 envelope unflavored gelatin

¼ cup cold water

¾ cup hot water

¾ cup bottled grape juice

2 tablespoons lemon juice

1 teaspoon liquid no-calorie sweetener

¼ teaspoon salt

Soften gelatin in cold water. Dissolve in hot water; add grape juice, lemon juice, sweetener, and salt; chill until syrupy. Beat thickened gelatin with rotary beater until it almost doubles in volume. Spoon into 1-quart mold; chill until firm.

LEMON GELATIN
(Makes 4 servings)
Zero calories

1 envelope unflavored gelatin

¼ cup cold water

1½ cups hot water

1/3 cup lemon juice

1½ teaspoons liquid no-calorie sweetener

Dash salt

Soften gelatin in cold water. Dissolve in hot water; add lemon juice, sweetener, and salt. Pour into one-pint mold; chill until firm.

LEMON-SHERRY DRESSING
(Makes 1/3 cup)
Zero calories

¼ cup lemon juice

2 tablespoons sherry wine

1 teaspoon liquid no-calorie sweetener

⅛ teaspoon salt

Combine all ingredients in small jar with screw top. Shake well before using. Serve on fruit salads.

LEMON MIST
(Makes 6 servings)
25 calories per serving

1 envelope unflavored gelatin

¼ cup cold water

1½ cups hot water

2 egg yolks, slightly beaten

1½ teaspoons liquid no-calorie sweetener

Dash of salt

¼ cup lemon juice

1 teaspoon vanilla

2 egg whites, stiffly beaten

Soften gelatin in cold water. Dissolve in hot water; stir gelatin mixture into egg yolks; add sweetener and salt. Pour mixture into top of double boiler; cook over simmering water, stirring constantly, about 5 minutes or until mixture coats spoon; remove from heat; add lemon juice and vanilla; chill until syrupy. Fold beaten egg whites into thickened gelatin mixture; spoon into 1-quart mold or 6 individual molds, 2/3 cup size. Chill until firm.

MADRILENE
(Makes 5 servings)
50 calories per serving

4½ cups (2 1-pint, 2-ounce cans) tomato juice

1 medium-sized onion, chopped

¼ cup green pepper, chopped

¼ cup celery stalks and leaves, chopped

2 teaspoons liquid no-calorie sweetener

2 tablespoons lemon juice

1 teaspoon salt

½ teaspoon paprika

1 bay leaf

2 envelopes unflavored gelatin

Combine 4 cups of tomato juice, onion, green pepper, celery, lemon juice, sweetener, salt, paprika, and bay leaf in medium-sized saucepan; simmer, covered, 30 minutes. Press mixture through sieve. Soften gelatin in remaining ½ cup tomato juice; add to hot mixture; stir until dissolved. Measure; add cold water to make 4 cups liquid; chill until firm. Serve cold; garnish with lemon slice.

ORANGE-TAPIOCA PUDDING
(Makes 6 servings)
85 calories per serving

1 egg yolk, slightly beaten

2 cups skim milk

3 tablespoons quick-cooking tapioca

⅛ teaspoon salt

1 egg white, beaten, but not dry

½ teaspoon vanilla

1 teaspoon liquid no-calorie sweetener

1¾ tablespoons sugar

3 medium oranges, peeled and sectioned

Mix egg yolk with milk in medium-sized saucepan; add tapioca and salt. Cook over medium heat, stirring constantly, 5 to 8 minutes or until mixture comes to a boil. Spoon small amount of hot tapioca mixture onto egg white in medium-sized bowl; blend; lightly blend in remaining tapioca mixture and vanilla.

Spoon 1 cup pudding into separate small bowl; add no-calorie sweetener; blend thoroughly; chill. Blend sugar into mixture remaining in medium-sized bowl; chill. Blend two mixtures together; chill. Serve garnished with orange sections and sprigs of fresh mint if desired.

LIME-MELON MOLD
(Makes 6 servings)
25 calories per serving

1 envelope unflavored gelatin

¼ cup cold water

1 cup hot water

½ cup lime juice

2¼ teaspoons liquid no-calorie sweetener

Dash of salt

2 cups small melon balls

Soften gelatin in cold water in medium-sized bowl; add hot water to dissolve gelatin. Stir in lime juice, sweetener, and salt; chill until syrupy. Fold in melon balls. Spoon into 6 individual molds, 2/3 cup size, or into 1-quart mold. Chill until firm.

√ COFFEE WHIP
(Makes 6 servings)
Zero calories

1 envelope unflavored gelatin

½ cup cold water

1½ cups hot strong coffee

1 tablespoon liquid no-calorie sweetener

½ teaspoon vanilla

Dash of salt

Soften gelatin in cold water. Dissolve in hot coffee; add sweetener, vanilla, and salt; chill until syrupy. Beat thickened gelatin with rotary beater until it almost doubles in volume. Spoon into sherbet glasses; chill until firm.

CLAM-TOMATO COCKTAIL
(Makes 6 servings)
12 calories per serving

2 cups canned or bottled clam juice

2¼ cups (1-pint, 2-ounce can) tomato juice

1 bay leaf

¼ teaspoon onion salt

Handful of celery tops

Slice of lemon

Combine all ingredients in medium-sized saucepan. Bring to boiling point; simmer 5 minutes to blend flavors; strain; chill. Serve cold, garnished with lemon wedges or chopped parsley.

CUCUMBER COCKTAIL
(Makes 1 serving)
Zero calories per serving

1 medium-sized cucumber, diced

2 tablespoons lemon juice

¼ cup water

¼ teaspoon onion salt

¼ teaspoon celery salt

¼ teaspoon salt

3 drops liquid no-calorie sweetener

Dash of pepper

Combine all ingredients; blend about 2 minutes, or until smooth, in electric blender; strain; chill. Garnish with dash of paprika.

Begin your meal with vegetable salad or clear broth. It takes the edge off your appetite.

SALAD SOUP
(Makes 6 servings)
12 calories per serving

1 clove garlic

3 small tomatoes, diced

½ cup celery, sliced

1 tablespoon vinegar

1 tablespoon lemon juice

1 teaspoon monosodium glutamate

½ teaspoon salt

Dash of pepper

Paprika

2¼ cups (1-pint, 2-ounce can) tomato juice

6 green onions, sliced (or 1 tablespoon chopped chives)

Rub medium-sized bowl with garlic. Discard garlic. Combine remaining ingredients in bowl. Chill 3 hours to blend flavors. Spoon into bouillon cups.

HEARTY VEGETABLE SOUP
(Makes 10 cups)
95 calories per cup

1 pound beef chuck (with all fat removed and cut into small pieces)

3½ cups water

1 teaspoon salt

Pepper to taste

¾ cup onion, diced

2/3 cup celery, diced

½ cup raw potato, diced

¾ cup carrot, diced

2 cans (1 pound each) tomatoes

Add water and seasonings to the beef chuck; simmer until meat is tender, about 1½ hours. Add the prepared vegetables, and cook until they are tender, about 25 minutes.

MINTED BUTTERMILK SOUP
(Makes 2 servings)
85 calories per cup

2 cups buttermilk

1 cup cucumber, finely diced

1 tablespoon fresh mint, chopped

2 teaspoons chives, chopped

Salt to taste

Dash of nutmeg

Combine ingredients in medium-sized bowl; chill. Serve cold; garnish with sliced strawberries, blueberries, or raspberries, if desired.

CHICKEN GUMBO SOUP
(Makes 8 servings)
25 calories per serving

4 chicken bouillon cubes

4 cups boiling water

8 cups water

¼ cup raw rice

1 can (about 1 pound) tomatoes

1 cup okra, sliced

½ cup cooked or frozen corn kernels

¼ cup onion, finely chopped

1 teaspoon celery salt

1 teaspoon salt

¼ teaspoon crushed red pepper

Dissolve bouillon cubes in boiling water in 4-quart saucepan; add water; bring
to boil. Pour rice slowly into boiling mixture; add remaining ingredients. Simmer,
covered, about 30 minutes or until vegetables are tender. Serve piping hot;
garnish with pinch of gumbo file powder in each serving if desired.

MUSHROOM SOUP, COUNTRY STYLE
(Makes 4 servings)
50 calories per cup

2½ cups skim milk

1 medium-sized onion, finely chopped

1 cup mushrooms, chopped

¼ teaspoon salt

¼ teaspoon celery salt

¼ teaspoon paprika

Scald milk and onion in top of double boiler. Add mushrooms and seasonings;
cook about 20 minutes or until mushrooms are tender. Serve hot; garnish with
chopped parsley and mushroom slices.

RUSSIAN BORSCHT

Dissolve 4 boullion cubes in 4 cups boiling water; cook with ½ cup grated
raw beets in covered saucepan for 15 minutes; cool and chill. Add 2 tablespoons
lemon juice just before serving. Salt and pepper to taste and garnish with thin
cucumber slice.

TOMATO-CELERY SOUP

Dissolve 2 bouillon cubes in 2 cups boiling water in a medium-sized saucepan.
Add 1 cup finely diced celery, ¼ cup finely chopped onion, 1 cup tomato juice,
salt and pepper to taste. Simmer until vegetables are tender. Serve hot.

191

ALPHABETICAL INDEX

192